CARVEL DAZE

A mischievous kid in the hippie generation speaks

Chris Garcia

Edited by Molly Spain
Managing editor, Sharon Pepper

CARVEL DAZE

A mischievous kid in the hippie generation speaks

Copyright © Chris Garcia (2022)

All rights reserved. No part of this publication may be reproduced, stored in a retrieval system, or transmitted, in any form or by any means, without prior written permission of the publisher.

ISBN: 978-0-578-33111-9

Published by Cloud Rider Productions
Requests to publish work from this book should be sent to:
chris@cloudriderproductions.com

Wichita Lineman
Words and Music by Jimmy Webb
Copyright © 1968 UNIVERSAL-POLYGRAM INTERNATIONAL PUBLISHING, INC.
Copyright Renewed
All Rights Reserved Used by Permission
Reprinted by permission of Hal Leonard LLC

Cover design: Mackenzie Lee

Printed by Amazon KDP Print

www.cloudriderproductions.com

Contents

Acknowledgments	1
Introduction	3
My First Friend	5
The Red Barn	12
Mom & Dad	23
Bayland Park	34
Baseball	41
Church	49
Big Girls & Little Girls	55
The Boys	61
The Locust Hunt	67
Popsicle Man!	71
Grandma Garcia	74
Charlie Brown	81
The Paper Route	93
Go Fly a Kite	100
Danger, Will Robinson!	104
Buster Willis and The Jump	107
Walk Like a Man	112
The Pinewood Derby	117
The Birth of Fire God	120

The Institution	125
Tricks & Treats, Night & Day	132
Christmastime	144
The End of the Innocence	160
Epilogue	165
Carvel Daze Songs Playlist Disc 1	170
Carvel Daze Songs Playlist Disc 2	171

Acknowledgments

The credit for this book goes to my brothers and sisters, who have encouraged me for years to write it, beginning with Sharon who prompted me to finally put it in motion and acted as managing editor and publisher during this entire process. No wonder she's a life coach. Then again, if the book sucks, it's my siblings' fault.

I would also like to credit Jordan Peterson, whom I've never met, for his books and lectures I followed during the writing of this book, which encouraged and edified me in so many ways. His "12 Rules For Life" are transformational.

This book is dedicated to Mom and Dad, to Grandma Garcia, and especially to my brothers and sisters who make up "The Crazy 8s!," and who have always lifted me in prayer.

God bless.

Chris Garcia

Introduction

I grew up in Houston, Texas, the middle kid in a large white family with an Hispanic last name, living in the same house with two parents, a Mexican cook, and a flying dog. I was the fifth in a lineup of eight kids, with three sisters and one brother ahead of me, and two sisters, a brother, and the dog behind me. In our house, at any given time, music would be playing, girls would be dancing, fires would be breaking out, kids would be falling out of moving vehicles, and Santa might even be threatening me on the phone. The cook taught life lessons with a flyswatter and the dog learned to fly without a cape or a bong. Things were weird like that on Carvel Lane in the 1960s.

The decade got off to a bad start with the assassination of John F. Kennedy. Some say that America's hopes and innocence died with him, and that was definitely true for some. His death certainly sent this country into a spiral of changes. But for us kids on Carvel Lane the sun still rose in the east and set in the west, and we knew how to fill the hours in between. Perhaps this story will show that for some of us, that innocence hadn't quite yet been laid to rest.

This book is titled after a double disc music mix I made for my brothers and sisters over a dozen years ago. Music was like another family member in our house and that mix seemed to capture our time together. We played it at a family party once, and after the vino got keeno we started singing together, and then we got up and danced with each other around the living room. Someone stood on an ottoman and another on the coffee table to play solos on air guitar and drums. It was a total geek-fest. This lasted for over an hour, and it was the only dance party we ever had together—it was also the last time I ever danced.

I've shared some of my essays with family members over the years, and after I made that music mix some of them began encouraging me to write about that time in our family history. Telling that story had been something I'd been considering, and while the title was obvious to me, I didn't think I had enough memories with the necessary details to fill a book. Then one day my sister Sharon asked me point-blank if I thought I could write the book; then she asked if I would; then she volunteered to take care of the business end; and the rest is, well, Carvel Daze.

To any kid who might be reading this, I do not recommend doing the things I write about in this book. Attempting the things we did without practice would be like calling yourself a lion tamer and walking into a circus cage. You will get hurt. It's not a question of bravery, it's just that you haven't been properly trained . . . yet. And while this book is about growing up in a house as one of "The Crazy 8s!," the story really begins with a friend.

My First Friend

I have a vivid memory of the day I met my very first friend. Think about that. I wonder how many people have even tried to think all the way back to the beginning of their remembrances, to their first friend, or to the day they actually *met* their first friend. I wonder how many of those people would be able to conjure a lucid memory of that first encounter. I thought about that moment only recently myself, and it wasn't hard for me to draw up that day at all, but I was surprised that I had never actually thought about him in that way before—as my very first friend—probably because he's been one of my closest friends ever since that day we met, and one of the best people I've ever known. My first friend's name is Bob Layton, and I remember the day we met.

When we moved from Kansas City to Houston in the spring of 1967, I was six years old. I don't have a lot of memories of Kansas City, at least none that involved playing with other kids. We had a neighbor that lived behind us named David Learner. He was a little older than I was, around the same age as my brother Dave. The only recollection I have of David Learner was the time his wiener dog went after our tomcat Smoky. Big mistake. Chain-link fences and an alley separated our backyards. I have an image of him shortly after the fight between the pets. It was in the fall, the trees were dark and getting bare, and the ground was covered with brown, wet leaves. David Learner was in his backyard close to the fence, crying as he held his dog like one would cradle a baby, with its paws in the air and its bloodied stomach exposed. The wounds were superficial, and the dog was okay, but if David Learner was ever our friend, I doubt that he was after that incident. Other than him, my only Kansas City memories of other human interaction involved my immediate family, and my cousins who were all much older than I.

It was a sunny afternoon the day we moved to Houston, and because there were eight kids in our family, we were expanding from a one-story house in KC to a two-story. The house seemed huge! And it had a staircase and a second floor! Some of the floors were tiled, and the wooden ones looked like they'd been dipped in honey. It wasn't a new house, but it sure looked new to me.

Bob lived three houses down on the same side of the street as we did. I didn't see him riding his red bike with training wheels up the sidewalk towards our house that day, but my sisters who were outside described that scene later. He was a curious kid, and one who was always looking for adventure, so he rode with determination and a purpose. He was coming to see who moved into the neighborhood.

There was no furniture in the house that I recall, at least there wasn't any in the living room yet, so as I was on my knees helping to unload boxes, I looked up to see a red-headed kid with his nose mashed into our screen door. We had a short, built-in bookcase just inside the doorway blocking part of his view so he asked whomever he saw if there were any kids in the house that could come out and play. My older sister Cindy looked at me and opened the door, and I got up and went outside. We introduced ourselves to each other and ended up sitting on the porch just talking. I don't remember what we were talking about, but a short time after he arrived a green, wood-paneled station wagon crossed the street in front of our house and pulled into the driveway next door. In the backseat of that car was another kid who looked to be around the same age as Bob, but a kid that would rub me the wrong way from that day on. I'll tell you more about him later.

Bob was one of two boys belonging to Jack and Susan Layton, who arrived from Oregon several years earlier. He was a little over a year younger than I was, and his older brother Bill was slightly older than my brother Dave. The two of them couldn't be any different. While Bob was good-natured, amicable, and funny, Bill . . . well, he was a good guy, but he had a little junkyard dog in him. The first time I played football against Bill, I knew I wasn't in Kansas anymore.

Bob and I became fast friends, and before long we were spending the night at each other's houses. Staying at his house was different for me because he had a TV in his room, plus he had a record player and had already started collecting comic books. Everything we needed was right there in his room, and he shared it all. We were already collecting 45s by then, so while we read his comic books, we'd be listening to music from the Monkees, Tommy James & The Shondells, Johnny Cash, one-hit wonders like *Vehicle* by the Ides of March or *Raindrops Keep Fallin' on My Head* by B. J. Thomas. And then of course, there was this band called The Beatles. But one of our favorites to spin was the comedy album *Revenge* by Bill Cosby. We played that album over and over until we had it memorized word for word. We used to walk down the street together, tossing a ball back and forth and trying out our comedy routines on one another, or we'd just recite it together.

On Saturday afternoons, after our cartoons had already played out, if there was a good monster movie coming on, we'd shut the blinds to make Bob's bedroom as dark as possible and watch *Creature From the Black Lagoon, Frankenstein, The Wolfman, Dracula,* or *The Mummy*. They absolutely terrified us. After an hour and a half of that dark horror, we'd have the full-on heebie-jeebies, so as soon as the movie ended, we'd throw the shutters open to watch reruns of *The Lone Ranger* or *The Cisco Kid,* or we'd just bolt for the outdoors and into the sunshine, where monsters never went.

But when it got late, we'd have to turn the music off. So we'd move into the living room to watch *The Late Show*. This was a weekend movie feature that aired at 10:30 p.m., after the 10:00 PSA that stated: "It's ten o'clock. Do you know where your children are?" That spooky message always set an ominous tone, putting our heads on a swivel as we scanned that darkened living room, looking for something lurking in the shadows. After the PSA, came the ten o'clock news. Bob's mom would usually make us a root beer float just before the movie, so with his parents having gone to bed, we'd settle in.

On one occasion we watched a movie called *The Defiant Ones* with Sidney Poitier and Tony Curtis. In the film they were two escaped prisoners on the run but chained together, one black and the other white, so they had to learn to work together to make their escape. At the end of the film, after the two had failed to hop a train and get away, they waited for a policeman to take them away as Poitier sang a chain gang song that ended the movie. The final four words of that song were, "Bowling Greee-*een*! Sewing machine!" And he sang it with a huge smile on his face. The next day Bob and I were walking down the street arm-in-arm, with one of us calling out, "Bowling Greee-*een*!" And the other answering, "Sewing machine!" Neither one of us knew what it meant, we just liked saying it.

During another late-night movie, we made too much noise and woke Bob's dad, a gruff, hardworking man from the steel mills who had no appreciation for being awake that late. He came out and said, "Chris, go home." Trembling like the Cowardly Lion who just got booted by The Wizard, I quickly gathered my things and went out the door. I knew Bob was in trouble, but I knew I couldn't help him. He was doomed. Besides, I had troubles of my own to deal with now. As I made my way back home it occurred to me that it was past 10:00, and my parents didn't know where *I* was.

While Bill was the more athletic of the Layton boys, Bob was more imaginative and creative. I suspect his interest in comic books and love of cartoons had a lot to do with that. He had a rock bed in an outdoor atrium that was part of his front porch. That was one of the focal points of our playtime. If we were playing with army men or miniature action figures, we were playing "mans," and if we were playing with our Matchbox cars or Hot Wheels, we were playing "cars." If we ever grabbed our guns and headed for Bob's treehouse, we played "war." I guess we tried not to make things too complicated. But Bob was great at making sound effects for everything, for cars peeling around corners in a chase, for fists punching faces in a fight, or for tanks blowing up in battle. In everything he did he was making his own little movie scene. One time, when we were in the yard timing each other running from one driveway to another, my sister Sharon saw that as Bob ran, he was looking back over his shoulder towards the ground. That was unusual, so she asked me why he was running that way, but I knew, because I *knew* him, so I told her: he was looking to see if he was kicking up any dust, like in the cartoons.

I remember one time Bob's parents took us to AstroWorld for his sixth birthday. Located across the freeway from the Astrodome —the first domed stadium ever built and nicknamed the Eighth Wonder of the World—AstroWorld was Houston's version of Six Flags Over Texas and was a legendary amusement park in its own right. So, on Bob's sixth birthday, we rode on The River Of No Return, a boat ride that sat approximately twenty people and snaked through and beneath a swampy canopy of moss-draped trees that filtered the sunlight into shadows, the sounds of birds and growling animals hidden somewhere behind them. The boat's guide made Bob the honorary captain of the ship, and towards the end of the ride we turned a corner and up in the near distance I saw that we were heading for a big dark tunnel with a waterfall pouring over its mouth. At that moment the guide cried out, "Oh no, Captain Bob! We're headed for the waterfall! What are you going to do?" He put the microphone in front of Bob's mouth and with both hands gripping the wheel and a steely determination in his eyes Bob looked straight ahead and said, "I'm going to drive right through it." I wouldn't be here to tell the story today if he didn't.

Bob had a great setup and the best toys, and playing with him at his house was always fun. But there was a big red house down the street, full of kids, that offered a few thrills and chills of its own.

Chris Garcia

The Red Barn

Our house on Carvel Lane was a ranch style, two story in one of America's first master planned communities built in the late 1950s and early 1960s, called Sharpstown. The very first suburb in Houston, and built with the hope of enticing the astronauts, Sharpstown was still a fairly new development when we moved here in 1967 and featured the first fully air-conditioned mall in the city. The astronauts ended up living further south, closer to NASA, and by the time we arrived our neighborhood, an island carved out of rice fields, was entering into a state of transition as it began to leave the black-and-white nostalgia of the fifties and wander into the new age colors of the sixties. Located ten miles southwest of downtown Houston, in its early years Sharpstown was a place where you might expect to see the ghosts of Tom and Huck sitting on a fence, chewing tobacco and whittling on sticks while some poor kid painted the pickets down below them. The spirit of those two intrepid adventurers lingered awhile but eventually faded out as the times and our neighborhood transformed into something new.

The exterior of our house was constructed with brown and red brick on the front of the lower level and the rest of the first story was fashioned with striated shingle siding. The second story was all wood. The house was painted red with white trim and after we moved in, we quickly learned that the kids on our block had already named it The Red Barn.

The interior of the house had four equal sized bedrooms on the right side of the house, two above and two directly below them, with bathrooms between each. There was no master bedroom and I still have no idea why. The living room was 12' x 17' with oak floors, and as you entered through the front door, if you looked left, you would find an open extension to the room that most people might have used for a dining area. That was where Dad had his desk and where Mom had her piano. There was a pocket door in that little room leading into the kitchen. The living room led directly into what would normally have been considered a den. That was our dining room, and it was roughly the same size as the living room. Another pocket door separated those two rooms and directly ahead and at the end of the dining room was a sliding glass door that led to the backyard. The kitchen was to the left of the dining room with a door that led to the garage. The dining room had a tiled floor and wood-paneled walls, and at the end of the wall on the right was an opening to a concealed stairway leading to the second floor.

My three older sisters—Vicki, Cindy, and Gayle—occupied the first-floor bedroom that faced the front of the house. That room was approximately 12' x 14' with bunk beds. My grandmother occupied the room that faced the backyard. Her room was slightly smaller. A full bathroom separated the two bedrooms. The rooms above them were the exact same size. I shared the larger room with my older brother Dave and younger brother Landry, and we also slept on bunk beds. My two younger sisters Sharon and Lisa occupied the smaller room directly above Grandma's room. Where did my parents sleep? In the living room, on a sleeper sofa, the kind with steel bars running across their backs. They slept there for five years, until they added two large rooms upstairs and moved into the master.

I offer up these details so that you might imagine three adults and eight kids ranging from ages one to thirteen—eleven(!) people in all—crammed together in a house that had less than 1,500 square feet of living space. That was the very definition of chaos.

Large families like ours, usually unheard of today, were a rarity even back then. When we moved to Houston there were only two other families like ours in the entire neighborhood, and because we kids seldom ventured beyond our own street in those early years, those families may as well have been living in other countries. We knew their last names because we all went to the same church, and our individual families nearly occupied entire pews, but beyond that they were strangers to us. For the people who lived on our block, we must have been a curiosity. A white family with eight kids and an Hispanic last name and a live-in Spanish-speaking grandmother who looked like a historic photograph of a small, white-haired Native American woman. But while we were moving into a new house and a new neighborhood, we were also moving into new times and a new era.

We saw a lot of history in just a short seven-year window when we were all still living together in that house. The sixties was a decade of intense change, some for the good and some not. It was certainly one of the most tumultuous times in US history.

The country was still experiencing the aftershock of JFK's assassination in 1963 and the ripple effects were both deep and wide, more like a tidal wave caused by the cultural and political shifting of tectonic plates following his death. The footing was uncertain and nobody knew where or how our nation would land. Two months after we left Kansas City, Muhammed Ali stood before the draft board in downtown Houston, a dozen miles away from our new house, and refused induction into the army. One year later Martin Luther King was assassinated. Exactly one week after that, the Civil Rights Act of 1968 was signed into law by LBJ and two months after that Robert Kennedy was assassinated. In December of that year I sat on the floor of my grandmother's room and had my world rocked as she and I watched a leather-clad Elvis Presley perform his televised '68 Comeback Special, where he closed with, "If I Can Dream," a powerful and moving tribute song to MLK that he sang in response to the assassination of RFK. One year later, as a family, we huddled on the wooden floor of our living room and witnessed, with bated breath, our three American astronauts making history's first landing on the moon and watched as Neil Armstrong took that "one giant leap for mankind." Two months later it was the Woodstock Music Festival in New York, a three-day outdoor concert attended by a half a million people in what would become one of the greatest musical events in history, and a watershed moment in the decade's counterculture movement. That same year launched *Sesame Street*, possibly the most influential children's television show ever produced, and *The Brady Bunch*, a new spin on the nuclear family. There were civil rights protests and anti-war riots all over the country, where people were beaten and cities were burned; the Cold War put a chill on the nation and the Vietnam War heated it up; and the music scene was being heavily influenced by a new generation of rockers and poets, birthing a new breed of rebellious teenagers, called hippies, many of whom ushered in a new age of drug use and experimentation. For them the war was out, man, and peace, free love, and flower power were in! And The Beatles were right in the middle of it, talking about a "Revolution," well you know. . . . And in that mix was a psychedelic gonzo journalist, Hunter S. Thompson, a lone wolf howling in the desert, who wrote about his drug-addled fears and loathings for the fate of America in *Rolling Stone* Magazine. Then in 1972, the news of Watergate broke, exposing a clandestine political scandal involving a sitting president. That tidal wave of change following JFK's death swept some things away into the bye and bye, and cleansed some others that needed to be purged. Still, there was plenty of debris left behind. It truly was the best of times and the worst of times.

In the midst of our nation's chaos, we made new friends and created our own little world of youthful chaos. The great thing for our friends, who all came from mostly two- and three-kid families, was that there was always activity at our house. Because of our age differences it was like we all took shifts, so night or day the lights were always on because there was always something to do and always something going on. It was easy for a neighborhood kid to cut loose at our house because it was always noisy and because it was easy to get lost in the crowd of our family. Heck, it was easy to get lost just sitting at our dining table!

After we'd been in the house a few years Grandma's reputation for her cooking, especially her Mexican food, grew, so having kids over at "supper time" was normal. Surrounded by ten other family members, sometimes my dad wouldn't even realize we had a guest at the table until they spoke.

Our dining table nearly occupied all of the space in our dining room. And actually, it wasn't a dining table at all but rather a wood-grained laminate conference table that did not match the darker paneling on the walls. My dad bought it from a neighbor at a garage sale a block away from our house. You don't start collecting antiques when you have eight kids, so there we were one Saturday afternoon, my dad and six of us walking this 5' x 9' conference table down the sidewalk towards our house, like army ants marching a giant stick back to their bed. The table was so big that we had to set it against the wall to the right, the one that concealed the stairway. In the evening we'd pull it out to the center of the dining room to make room for us all to sit for dinner. There were folding chairs tucked away in a closet somewhere and they'd come out for dinner time as well.

Dinner for us was a time to sit together as a family. That wasn't just a rule, it was our way of life so there was no negotiating out of it, unless Mom was cooking liver. At the first whiff of that meat, I'd head straight to Bob's to see what they were having for dinner. What kind of sick mind ever conceived of liver as being edible, and who ever presented the notion that it was a good idea to eat a filter anyway?

Grandma usually cooked dinner but occasionally Mom would take a shift. Mom had a few signature dishes that she did well and was otherwise a good cook when she wanted to be ("when she wanted to be" being the operative qualifier). Where a grill master will tell you to smoke it low and slow, my mom was a firm believer in high and dry. Crank it to 500 and pull it out when the fire department shows up. If we didn't happen to see her when she got home from work, her meal presentation was usually a good indicator of her mood. Oh, the things she could do with meat when she wasn't happy! One time she gaveled dinner to order using what appeared to be a petrified turkey leg. Another time she set her pot roast on the table for dinner, and I mistakenly asked her when I could have my baseball glove back. This type of humor did not improve her mood. As it turned out, my glove was more tender, and I imagined, easier to digest. But I didn't tell her that. It was her rendition of liver, however, that was the most memorable.

First of all, there's no possible way to make liver taste good. And no, not even sautéed onions and garlic helped. Liver is so bad that not even Grandma Garcia would make a run at it. All I know is, whoever taught my mom how to prepare that abomination should have been convicted of a hate crime. It was so bad that our dog, Charlie Brown, wouldn't even attempt to come inside the house. One night, when I made it home just before dinner, I got snared. I opened the front door and smelled that wretched odor that instantly closed my throat, but it was already dark outside, and too late for me to make a break for it. No way I could get to Bob's house in time. I was trapped. But that night was to be the last night of liver for me. That night, my mom and I had a showdown.

The meal started with the entire family and ended with just me at the table. I tried to eat the liver, but it smelled like it was still inside the animal, and it tasted the same way. I've never since put anything in my mouth that had the consistency of compressed sawdust, like liver does. I took one bite and it made me gag, but she was watching me and made it clear that she was having none of that. She told me I was not allowed to leave that table until I'd, "cleaned my plate." And so I tried all the classic kid moves; I tried cutting some of it into small pieces and mingling it with the vegetables; I tried burying some under the mashed potatoes; I put some pieces in my napkin and stuffed that under my leg; I would have slow fed our dog but he was hiding in the backyard. What still remained I tried dressing up with ketchup. No help. I tried topping it with sliced grapes. Still gagging. So I sat there as the time slowly ticked away. First it was thirty minutes, then it was an hour, then it was two hours, and then two of my sisters graduated high school. But I did not relent. I sat there until the lights were out, everybody went to bed, and the house was completely quiet. Eventually my mom came back to the dining room, accepting defeat, and told me to "clean my plate" and go to bed. As I lifted my plate and left the table, I wondered why I didn't toss it in the garbage the first time she said it.

In our house I was always slow to get out of bed on Monday through Friday of the school year, but on Saturdays I was somehow up and energized at the crack of dawn. Some of us had to be up in time to eat breakfast and to watch our favorite cartoons. For Houston in 1968 there were only the three network channels and PBS, and that was it for TV. So we were up to watch *The Archies*, *Wacky Races*, *The Flintstones*, and *The Banana Splits*. This was still during the dawning of the popularity of Saturday morning television, which would extend until the afternoon with *Batman*, *Fantastic Four*, *Underdog*, *Shazzan!*, *George of the Jungle*, and *Jonny Quest*. I would be at Bob's house early to watch television in his room but if we got tossed out of there for disturbing the peace we would head back to my house, through the front door, either under or over my parents sleeping on the foldout sofa, with the always cheerful, "Good morning, Mr. and Mrs. Garcia!" coming from Bob, and into the dining room where the TV was. Zero consideration was given to the two exhausted adults trying to sleep in the room we'd just infiltrated. But the living room, the dining room, and the kitchen were the high-traffic areas in our house. Those were the common areas that you had to walk through to get to your room. And in the far corner of the dining room was where you turned that dark corner that led upstairs.

That hidden stairway was a source of fascination to all kids who came into our house, for several reasons: one, there was only one other house on our block that had a second story and they had no kids, so nobody had ever been in there; two, because the stairway was hidden by the wall you wouldn't know it was there unless you looked for it, or unless somebody showed you where it was; and three, because the stairway was usually dark, you couldn't exactly see what was up there. Grandma Garcia would sometimes use that fear to tease us when we were young. "Better not go up there. Cucuy!" We didn't know what that meant but it sounded dark and sinister, so we stayed put. I understood this mystery more completely, and many years later, when my two-year-old nephew would hear an unexpected sound coming from upstairs, which got his immediate attention. He would then listen intently with head slightly cocked for another sound, then point his index finger up and say, monster! All visiting kids would ask to go up there, but they wouldn't ever attempt those stairs without an adult escort, or unless one of us Garcia kids took them.

Those stairs were a great source of entertainment for us as well. Sometimes we'd jump down the stairs just to see how many we could skip at one time. Jumping over five was about normal. Sometimes we'd put both hands on the rail and walk down on the opposite wall, skipping the stairs altogether. My brother Dave and I would use that stairway to stage fights, like stuntmen in a bar brawl, fake punching each other, complete with sound effects, as we rolled slow motion down the wooden stairs. But the best was when we'd polish the stairs, put pillows against the wall at the bottom landing and ride a sheet or blanket or sleeping bag down the stairs like a toboggan. Hey, if you don't have snow or can't afford to go to an amusement park, make your own! But that wasn't nearly the craziest thing we did in that house.

We had a two-car garage that my grandmother would occasionally hose down after sweeping to keep the dirt and dust away. Whenever she finished, she'd go back inside to watch her "stories." Once she got settled in, we'd follow up by dusting one side of the garage with laundry detergent; then we'd wet it down again with the hose and spread it all around with a broom to get it good and slick; then we'd ride in on our bikes from the street, up the driveway at full speed and as soon as we hit the front edge of the garage we'd slam on the brakes and lay our bikes down in a sideways skid, sliding across the polished concrete until we slammed into the washer and dryer. This particular event did not last too long before Grandma was out and after us with her flyswatter. But what we didn't realize back then was Grandma never reported what we did to Mom or Dad. She never busted us, at least not that I can recall, and we did truly stupid stuff like that on a regular basis. Our washer and dryer were literally running night and day, seven days a week, but the dents and scratches in those machines were never questioned and were never explained. Incredibly, they were never even mentioned.

Another favorite activity was to build a model car, fill it with lighter fluid, stick a firecracker in it, then light it and roll it down the driveway until it exploded and burst into flames, burning until it became just a black, molten blob of plastic goo that would eventually harden on the concrete. We just left it there. These things were happening all the time, and with eight kids at least half of us were always going to be guilty of something, but there was no prosecution, probably because my parents didn't have enough time or energy to even open the interrogation process. And these were just scenes from inside our house, or on our property. I look back now on what horrors our neighbors must have endured when we moved here and hit that neighborhood, swarming it like a scene out of *Lord of the Flies*. But because of that chaos, because of our numbers, and because of the house's intrigue, kids wanted to come to our place for adventure, and as they left their houses I would always hear them call out, "Hey Mom, we're going to The Red Barn!"

Mom & Dad

My dad's name is Joe Garcia. My mom's name is Mary Nolene Breting. Joseph and Mary. He was full-blooded Mexican, and she was of Irish/German/French descent. His skin was light brown and hers was alabaster white. They had eight kids. And yes, they were Catholic.

My father's parents were both Mexican born but he was born here in America in 1929, after his parents moved the family from Detroit to Kansas City, and less than two months after the stock market crash that launched the world into the Great Depression. His father, Santos, went back to Mexico looking for work when my dad was very young, but Santos was killed under mysterious circumstances while in Mexico, leaving Dad's mother to raise him and his three brothers and sisters on her own, taking whatever jobs she could get to raise and support her family. His older brother Damien would grow up to assume the responsibilities as the father figure in the house.

My dad was a Marine who served in Korea from 1950-1952. After South Korea had been overrun by the North Korean Army (NKA) he was deployed at age nineteen from Camp Pendleton in San Diego as part of the First Marine Division that made a daring surprise amphibious landing at Inchon, destroying the NKA there, then moving east across the peninsula to take back the occupied capitol city of Seoul. There the Marines advanced block by block, engaging in hand-to-hand street fighting to retake the city, then to Pusan and eventually combining with an Army division to advance north of the 38th parallel and into the Chosin Reservoir, where they fought in one of the most vicious battles in US military history. The Chinese army crossed into North Korea, outfoxing General MacArthur's strategy, and trapped the Marines, outnumbering them ten to one in a frozen, snow-covered mountainous terrain where temperatures dropped down to forty degrees below zero overnight. Those who didn't survive the conflict were either killed in combat or froze to death. I later read that the Chinese broke through the Marines' defenses and the fighting went hand to hand, with fixed bayonets. The Chinese hid by day and conducted their attacks like that every night for two weeks. Frozen bodies were stacked up and used as sandbags to help protect against those night raids. Against all odds the Marines fought their way out of that trap and somehow returned home to live out their lives as normally as possible. America did its best to forget that war, but the Marines didn't. Those survivors are revered in the Marine Corps today and will forever be known as the Frozen Chosen. My dad never talked about his time in Korea, and in our household, you were encouraged not to ask. He had a small almost imperceptible scar on his face that I asked my mom about one time. She said he got it in a fight while in the Marines, but that was all he ever told her.

Mom and Dad married while he was in the Corps so when Dad returned from the war, he got a job and took night classes until he finished college. Mom and their first three children, all girls, attended his graduation, along with Mom's parents. Several years after graduating Dad accepted a job selling chassis parts for Moog Automotive. He was a traveling salesman and proud to be a Moog Man. Eventually he and Mom grew the family to eight children and when the opportunity presented itself, he transferred from Kansas City to Houston, Texas, in 1967. He knew everything about the undercarriage of a car and was sent down to the Lone Star State to open up new territories in Oklahoma, Nebraska, Texas, Louisiana, and wherever else he could find business. His bosses' names were Mr. Bushyhead and Mr. Reamer. They sounded like cartoon characters to me. But seriously, who wants a boss named Reamer?

For the better part of our lives, Dad was gone five days a week traveling for his job, leaving town just about every Monday morning and returning home to us on Friday evening. When he traveled, he carried one large, grey hard-shell suitcase, a garment bag, and a large black briefcase for his parts catalogs and paperwork. As younger kids we would attack him when he came through the door on a Friday night, we were so happy to see him. We'd try to help him carry his stuff inside, but it was all very heavy, so we had to drag them into the house. He had this routine where he'd drop his loose change into his suitcase during the week so that when he came home and opened his suitcase on the bed we would dig for treasure in the corners as we helped him unpack. He wore a suit and tie to his sales calls, and he only had one or two suits at a time, so when we unpacked his suitcase, we were mostly unpacking his shirts. I'll never forget the smell of him in those shirts. It was his smell, the smell of sweat and aftershave, the smell of a hardworking man—that was the smell of my dad. But somehow it was more than just that. Unpacking his belongings felt like a rite of passage, like something of a bond, or maybe I was just getting a glimpse into my own future.

My mom put a musical instrument in almost all of her children's hands. For me she chose the trumpet. But first, I had to learn how to prove myself on the cornet, which, being shorter and more compact than a trumpet, was like a trumpet on training wheels. I'll never forget the first time she brought it home. I don't recall her ever asking me what instrument I wanted to play, and it was a surprise to me when she came home one day and handed it to me. I had just finished opening the case and trying to spit out a few notes when my dad walked through the front door and said, "What do you have there, son?" I didn't know so I shrugged my shoulders and handed it to him whereupon he brought the mouthpiece to his lips and proceeded to play taps perfectly, and for his encore he knocked out reveille without missing a note. He then handed it back to me, smiled, and headed for the kitchen.

He enjoyed doing similar things to all of his children. If he ever saw us pull a fresh apple out of the fridge he'd ask if he could have a bite. So, sure Dad, here, have a bite. He would take the apple and somehow round off his bite, snapping off at least half of that apple, and I mean with down-to-the-core precision. Then he would hand the demolished hunk of fruit with dangling seeds back to us and walk away. He was a funny guy. But he only got away with that stunt once with all of us.

As a boy I noticed that Dad's side of the family had darker skin than ours, but the only explanation I could come up with for that, or the only difference I could see between our families, was that my mom's skin was white. That's about as far as my observation went. That they were all full-blooded Mexican and we were half never registered and was never pointed out to me.

But the way we were raised was a little complicated. As the years passed, I learned that Dad grew up on the "wrong side of the tracks," and that sometimes he had to defend himself in fights with kids from other neighborhoods, kids with different skin colors. At dinner time he'd speak to his mother in Spanish, and I believe there was a brief time in my life when I could make out what they were saying, but he wasn't interested in having us learn Spanish. This was before Spanish was even considered a second language, but the reason he didn't want us speaking Spanish was that he didn't want his kids getting into fights just because people perceived us as being different.

Joe Garcia excelled at everything he did, despite being raised without a father. He was an exceptional student and a star athlete in three sports: baseball, football, and basketball. Several years ago, and getting towards the end of his life, two of my dad's childhood friends came to our house to visit him. This was a big occasion for all of us because we'd heard so little about his early life, and because we'd never seen his buddies before. We'd heard stories occasionally, but we'd never met them, so for us, and for him, this was a big deal and a special occasion for a family gathering. That evening, after a big meal, we gathered in the large living room and sat around as they told us Dad's story.

Dad was a straight-A student and a three-sport athlete. Apparently he was known beyond his own neighborhood because one day as he was sitting on the porch with his two best friends, Celso and Nicho, a priest from another parish came looking for him. He walked up to the porch and introduced himself to my dad and said that his church, Redemptorist, had an all-girls school that he wanted to integrate by introducing boys to the student body, and that he wanted to start an athletic program at the school as well. Apparently, he'd done his homework and asked around the area about an exemplary student and star athlete and my dad's name was mentioned. Well, they had the discussion and my dad agreed to attend his school but only on the condition that the priest accept his buddies as well. As Celso and Nicho told us, they were not good students and the priest didn't want to take them, but my dad said that he would only go if they came with him. The priest resisted but eventually acquiesced and the three of them ended up playing together on the Redemptorist High School football team where one school newspaper article described Dad as "one of the best all around backs in the city" and one who "never quits no matter what odds come his way." The three of them went on to graduate from Redemptorist, where my dad met my mom. Dad would go on to be accepted at MIT, but he chose the Marines instead. Celso went on to become a dentist, and Nicho became a surgeon. As they finished their stories, they credited Dad with their later success. That priestly visit turned out to be an opportunity of a lifetime, given to three poor boys from the wrong side of the tracks who all went on to graduate college and to lead very successful lives.

Grandma Garcia used to tell the story about the time the Chinese owners of the laundromat she worked for in Kansas City offered her money to buy my dad from her. That doesn't sound weird, right? But I guess they knew a winner when they saw one. I guess my mom did, too. The two of them ended up acting and singing together in one of their high school musicals. That would figure since they were practically living out *West Side Story*, or *Romeo and Juliet*.

My dad was not considered acceptable to some members of my mom's side of the family when she and Dad started dating, so he had to prove himself. After his time in Korea, but while he was still in the Marines and on leave, around age twenty-one, he was called by some of the men on Mom's side of the family to meet at one of their apartments in Kansas City. Ostensibly, they invited him over to just meet him and to get to know him, but maybe he was being summoned to be interviewed, as an intimidation tactic. After all, one of them was a cop. My dad told me this story six months before he died and said that he went to that meeting gladly and unafraid, that he was polite and respectful, answering all of their questions and left with their approval. Dad had his charm and he could not have gotten as far as he did without being street savvy and smart, and Mom's side of the family grew to love him. But I don't know what result those men expected in their little interrogation. Like a Marine who just walked out of the Chosin Reservoir could somehow be intimidated.

After that interview, it was pretty much game over. Mom and Dad got married.

"My mother had a great deal of trouble with me, but I think she enjoyed it." —Mark Twain

My mom was a renaissance woman. Born in Kansas City, she was the youngest of four children. She was the baby of the family, born thirteen years later than her sister Rosie, an "accident" as they used to say, but not a welcome accident by all in her family.

At the time of her birth her mother wasn't prepared for a new addition to the family, and early on, her older sister Rosie didn't like being displaced as the baby of the family, having held that title for thirteen years. But her dad doted on her. He was a big German man with a robust singing voice, and early on it became evident that she was an extremely gifted vocalist, a prodigy even. He encouraged her singing and when she became old enough, she began playing the organ and singing in the church choir with him. We have a 1954 church recording of them when she was a teenager on a 78 RPM red shellac album, which was how LPs were produced pre-vinyl—something I've never seen since. We also have studio recordings of her on a radio show, and on those records you can hear the talent.

She could have pursued a career as a trained operatic soprano but chose marriage and motherhood instead. Mother of eight, she was an independent thinker, a voracious reader, and one of the smartest people I've ever known. When we arrived in Houston, she had to get a job to help support her brood, so she went to work as an executive secretary for Esso, which later became Exxon, at the Humble Building downtown.

She was a walking encyclopedia of knowledge. For us she was the internet, before there was such thing as home computers. When we were kids, Mom could literally answer any question we had. Math, science, history—she had the answers. We took that knowledge for granted when we were young but as we grew older, we marveled at her ability. Of course, after she answered, she would tell us to go look it up for ourselves, not to check on her answers, but to get us into books, and looking into things on our own. She and Dad believed strongly in education, investing in a set of actual encyclopedias that were kept on a wooden stand in our living room, always accessible. All of us ended up pursuing higher education, with my two younger sisters earning doctorates and two of my older sisters holding master's degrees.

We had a mahogany-colored upright piano in our house, and during any break in the action Mom would always be at it, playing a song that fit her mood and singing along. She had books of sheet music and an album collection that, in quantity, would have rivaled any teenager's at the time. It included musicals like *Funny Girl*, *Showboat*, *The Sound of Music*, *Mary Poppins*, *West Side Story*, and *The Music Man*. She listened to the crooners, like Frank Sinatra, Tony Bennett, Nat King Cole, Rosemary Clooney, and Bing Crosby. There were albums by Burt Bacharach, Johnny Mathis, and Andy Williams, jazz from Louis Armstrong, Benny Goodman, the Count Basie Orchestra, and Ella Fitzgerald. She took my older sisters to see The Who's *Tommy*. And then there were all of the Christmas and opera albums. Music was always playing in our house, and it seemed like Mom knew the words to every song ever recorded because, if you were in the car riding along with her, she knew and sang every song that played on the radio. I don't remember ever talking to her in the car; I only remember listening to her sing. Music was in her DNA and singing was her therapy, her escape. And there was no chance that that music gene would escape her kids.

After I learned the trumpet and had played it for a few years Mom entered me into a UIL contest, which was sort of like a recital. She did it with all of us who played instruments. At the contest you had to answer a few questions about the piece you were going to play and then play it from memory with a UIL accompanist on piano. We were all given choices of music to practice and then we'd have to select one. After that, we'd practice every night with Mom playing piano, until we had it down. I played a piece called "El Torero" (The Bullfighter) and won whatever ribbon I was supposed to win. All of us kids who played an instrument did the same thing. Music was such a force in our family that my older sister Gayle became a professional musician, playing viola for the Houston Symphony, the Houston Grand Opera, and the Houston Ballet, and she still plays today.

I was born a natural left-hander, but my parents switched me to a righty when I was very young. I still did things left-handed as a kid and one day I asked my Mom why they switched me. She said that it was one of Dr. Spock's recommendations because the world, including school desks, was set up more for right-handed people. I didn't understand how he came to hold that kind of sway over them, but I thought it was pretty cool that decisions regarding my life were being influenced by *Star Trek*.

My mom also had a good sense of humor. One day she came home from work and told me this joke: "If the Houston Oilers moved to the Philippines, what would they be called?" I thought for a moment and told her I didn't know. She said, "The Manila Folders!" The Oilers were a perennial loser at that time, so I got the folder part, but the joke didn't make any sense to me. She was a smart lady so I couldn't figure out why she didn't know it was supposed to be *Vanilla* Folders. Far be it from me to correct her.

Another time, during a break in the music, she and I were alone in the house and I was walking through the dining room when I started mocking one of her favorite Frank Sinatra songs, altering the lyrics by singing out loud, drawing out the vibrato: "Stranger in the night, than in the morning. Stranger in the morning, than in the evening...." She cut right in, "Stranger in the evening, than any time at all!"

Looking back now, we were one of two families with an Hispanic surname in the neighborhood that I was aware of, but I'm not certain about that because I never made the distinction. I didn't realize my name was different or that I may be viewed differently until I was in the sixth grade. I just remember that I had pride in the Garcia name.

Chris Garcia

Bayland Park

For at least five years of my life, Bayland Park was the center of my universe. So many of my childhood memories are associated with that ballpark. Situated three blocks east of our house, where Carvel Lane dead ends, it contained multiple baseball fields for boys ranging from eight years old to sixteen years old, a softball field for the girls, and a football stadium for boys eight to twelve years old. There were no soccer fields because soccer hadn't been invented yet. It also had a covered pavilion area for parties with a playground right next to it. Back then you could access the fields any time, day or night. It was our social center, and the ultimate summer theater.

Bayland Park was bound by our neighborhood on its north and west sides, and by two busy streets on its south and east sides. There was an opening in the chain-link fence at the end of Carvel Lane that served as one of several entry points for the ballpark. The entry points from the neighborhood streets were narrow and ramped up through the entryway with a dirt slope that dropped into the park, so you either walked in, or you jumped the dirt ramp on your bike, landing on the asphalt street about six feet away. We only walked when we had to.

The trees in our neighborhood hadn't matured yet in the late sixties so, looking in that direction from a second-story window of our house at night, you could see the Conoco gas station sign at an intersection three miles away. C-O-N-O-C-O. CONOCO. And the Globe store. G-L-O-B-E. GLOBE. I must have been captivated by this technological breakthrough where signs could spell. But the best part of that vantage point was seeing the halo-like white glow of the ballpark on that not-too-distant horizon, and longing for it. When the window was open, and our windows were always open in the summertime, you could hear the roar of the crowd, which made me feel like I'd missed something. So I was always there. We were always there. Because that's where everything was happening, and we didn't want to miss anything.

In the late sixties and early seventies, every field at Bayland Park was used by at least six teams, so there were games going on at every field, every evening, except for Sundays. Some of the fields were so close to each other that you could watch the game from the backstop of one field and walk twenty-five feet to the outfield fence of an adjacent field to watch another game. Entire families would pack into their cars for one kid's game, brothers going to see brothers' games, sisters going to watch brothers' games, brothers going to see sisters' games, all the different age groups gathering together to roam and explore the park, so the place was always teeming with activity.

Entering Bayland Park was like walking into a carnival, or an amusement park. It was a sensory blast of sights, sounds, smells, and constant movement, just pure energy and excitement all around you. At night, every field with lights was lit. As you walked from one field to another you could see kids playing king of the mountain on a pile of sand; a cup ball game being played right next to it; six kids racing by to fetch a foul ball, which yielded a free snow cone upon return; girls gathered together around the backs of bleachers doing God knows what (who knows what girls do?); concession stands doing brisk business with people lined up three wide and three deep, the smell of hot dogs, popcorn, and cotton candy wafting through the entire park; announcers in the second story of the concession stands calling up the next batter. And man, that was it! Having your name called as the next batter up. Especially during the 8:00 games. Those were night games, under the lights! I lived for those night games. That was The Show!

Night games at Bayland Park. As the sky faded from dark blue to black and the evening surrendered to the night, the lights would blink on, and the atmosphere seemed to morph into something that felt like a change of dimensions. That's when the park transformed, as if the lights of every field slowly subdued themselves from a bright shine to a softer glow or a twinkle. Because half of the park remained unlit, the fields themselves became like individual stages where the uniforms became brighter, the grass looked deeper green, and the players came into sharper focus. Even the landscape changed. As the sun eased down shadows were cast, the moon rose up, and hiding places were revealed. It was a place to run away and be free with just your friends, at night! Girls went to those games to watch certain boys. Boys, when they didn't have a game, went to meet up with other boys, and some, who would never admit it, went to see certain girls. It was a nightly social event where kids played with their friends and went to other fields to see their other friends from other schools. We watched our older brothers play in the fields we would later grow into. Some of them stood out and developed reputations around the ballpark. Pretty girls went to see them play. They were the gods of the fields. We learned how to interact with kids of all ages, and artfully dodge adults. But parents were never too far away, so the park always felt safe and secure. There was no sense or fear of danger back then. So we were set free to roam, explore new horizons, and wonder.

Game Day. Things were different on Game Day. While the carnival was going on outside the fence line, inside the line it was all business. My sisters knew better than to try to talk to me on game day, even when I was in my room dressing for the game. That was a ritual unto itself. But nobody in my family approached me when I was inside that fence line. It was a different time and we had different ways. Nobody brought food or drinks to the players. Moms were not embarrassing their kids and Dads didn't coach or offer tips from behind the dugout. And nobody grieved the umpires. The managers and coaches were in charge and none of us wanted to be distracted. We were focused, and for me, I didn't have an interest in anything outside of the field I was playing on.

I didn't always have a ride home after my games so sometimes I had to walk home, even if it was 10:00 at night. That wasn't unusual. But God forbid we lose a game. When that happened, somehow word would reach home ahead of me. I later learned that my younger sisters would shut the curtains, dim the lights, and put on sackcloth before I got home, and when I entered the house, nobody said a word or even looked at me. The house was in mourning. I'd go straight to my room and shut my door and wouldn't come back out until the next day. At the end of every game, we shook hands with our opponents and told them, "good game" and I always did that without hesitation because we were trained to be good sportsmen. I just hated to lose.

We were not one of the families that packed into their car for the game. There were too many of us. The Big Girls were usually busy with their own lives, and Mom had to be home most evenings, but she came when she could, and when she did it was usually a surprise. I always looked for her in the stands at least once before the game and once during. My dad was usually out of town, so seeing him at one of my games was an even bigger surprise. Usually I heard him before I saw him. I'd be on the mound toeing the rubber when I'd hear him say, "C'mon babe, chuck it in there." I'd look to my side and there he'd be, leaning on the fence next to the gate that led to our dugout. Seeing my parents at games always energized me.

I started playing Little League baseball when I was eight years old. It was the first love of my life, and the longest lasting. As I got a little older, when I wasn't at the ballpark at night, I was there during the day. I didn't call my friends to get a game going. I barely used the phone at all. In our house it seemed like kids weren't even supposed to use the phone. It was used by adults, and my older sisters who were like adults. If I was ever caught using the phone it was assumed I had nothing better to do so I would be put to chores immediately. Phone? What's a phone? So to round up a game I'd just hop on my bike, which was like my horse, and ride around picking up guys around the neighborhood to get one going. Now understand, we didn't have gear bags with our own helmets, batting gloves, two types of fielders' gloves, and $300 bats forged out of the molten iron and nickel drilled from the earth's core, coated by the dust of Saturn's rings, and pulled out of and paid through Uranus, like today's kids. We had one glove each, looped onto our handlebars and at best, maybe we had two kids with bats. We usually only had one ball.

Seldom did we ever get enough guys to field entire teams. Usually we'd get out there with five or six and then meet up with another game and make a bigger game. We'd have about ten to twelve players, enough for a pitcher, a first baseman, two infielders, and one or two outfielders for each team. We had no catcher because we didn't have catcher's gear. The pitcher would throw a pitch at batting practice speed and a player from the opposing team would stand at the backstop to retrieve the pitched ball and throw it back to the pitcher. For right-handed batters the fielders would be on the left side with right field being closed, and for left-handed batters we'd shift to the right with the same rule for left field. And that's the way we played, from morning to dinner time.

We didn't wear shorts to play, ever. And we didn't have baseball pants either. The ones we had were issued by the league for game days only and had to be returned at the end of the season. You have to be ready to slide at all times when playing baseball, even when it's not necessary, so we played in our jeans and t-shirts, and we always wore the baseball caps of the teams we played for. I don't remember ever getting hungry, and when we got thirsty, we drank water out of the field hose. Occasionally we'd pool our meager funds and split a few donuts from the Shipley Donut shop across the street, but that was about it. There had to be a very good reason to break from the game.

The worst days were the ones when we had to delay the game because we lost a ball. When that happened, we rounded up our horses and scoured the neighborhood for empty soda bottles. They could be redeemed for maybe two cents or a nickel. Enough of them, and we could buy us a brand-new ball at the five-and-dime just a block away from the fields. There was nothing like opening the Rawlings box containing a brand-new baseball. You'd peel back the thin white wrapping paper and look inside to see the pure white leather ball with its raised red seams. Of course, the first thing I'd do is smell it, because that was one of the great smells of baseball. That, the smell of my oiled glove, and the smell of the grass in the field. Heaven. Then back to the fields, and back to the game. The only rule after that was to be home before suppertime. After supper, during the season, it was back to the ballpark, and back to those carnival lights.

Baseball

"The one constant through all the years, Ray, has been baseball. America has rolled by like an army of steamrollers. It's been erased like a blackboard, rebuilt and erased again. But baseball has marked the time. This field, this game: it's a part of our past, Ray. It reminds us of all that once was good and it could be again." —Terence Mann (*Field of Dreams*)

I played Little League baseball for five years until I moved up to Pony league at age thirteen. When I turned ten years old, I left the Pee-Wee division and entered tryouts for the very first time, with the hope of being drafted by a major league team. This was a highly anticipated event and a defining moment in any kid's baseball career as it was well known that the turnout would be huge and that all eyes, of both players and coaches from around the league, would be on you as you performed on that stage. It was an hour-long showcase of pressure-packed drills that put each kid's skill level on display, and for a ten-year-old coming out of Pee-Wees, it was a shot at The Bigs.

Signing up for tryouts and league play took place in early February, so it always seemed to be cold, grey, and wet on those days. We signed up at the concession stand of the main field, M-1, and coaches would be there scouting already, walking around with coffee steam curling up from the paper cups in their hands, or selling hot chocolate to the prospects from behind the concession stand counter, asking questions about the team they came from or the positions they preferred playing. Tryouts would be a few weeks later and the season would open for team practice shortly afterwards, in early March, so Dad took me to Oshman's Sporting Goods to buy me a new pair of cleats, my all-time favorite type of shoe. I'd grown out of my Pee-Wee glove so for my move up, he also let me pick out a new Rawlings fielders glove. The glove I decided on would likely turn out to be a three-year engagement, an eternity in kid years, so the selection process for me was the kid-equivalent of picking out a wife; I made my choice carefully. The gloves were displayed on a long wooden shelf, chest high to me, and I took my time to look at each individual glove, turning it over, testing the fit on my hand, bending it and shaping it, pounding the palm with my fist until I found the one I loved, and committed to it. I never said it had to love me back.

The first thing I did when I got home after that trip to Oshman's was lace up my new cleats, go to the front yard, and start running sprints to break them in, and to see how much faster I could run while wearing them. I wasn't looking behind me to see if I was kicking up any dust, but I was listening for the grass being torn up under my feet as I dug in with every step. Then Dad would come out to play catch and get my arm loose. I was throwing everything at ten years old, baseballs, footballs, rubber balls, rocks, chunks of overcooked liver, so getting loose took about two throws, but he was also starting the process of showing me how to break in my new glove.

While at Oshman's he'd bought some Neatsfoot oil so after throwing for about fifteen minutes we went inside and he cleaned the glove and showed me how to apply the oil, explaining that it would soften the leather and speed the process of breaking it in. As I slipped the glove on I instinctively brought it to my face to breathe in that new leather smell, the smell I imagined of the cowboy life of hard work and life outdoors, and methodically rubbed in the oil. I took my time and made sure that I did exactly as Dad instructed me, and from then on preparing my glove for the upcoming season became a solemn annual winter ritual. After that, he put a baseball in the glove pocket, folded the glove into place and wrapped a rubber band around it. Tryouts were three weeks away and he wanted me to be prepared so he told me to put the glove under my mattress and take it out after a week and start playing catch with it whenever I could.

The actual day of tryouts for the majors was intense. There was a lot of pressure to perform well because the competition at those events included kids ranging in ages from ten to twelve years old, so I was competing against other kids like myself who were moving up from Pee-Wees, as well as those eleven- and twelve-year-old kids who didn't make the majors the previous year and spent the season in the minors. The only open slots on a team in the majors were the ones vacated by the kids who were twelve years old the previous season, so there weren't very many roster spots to land on any team.

There were so many kids trying to make a team that the tryouts lasted from morning 'til early afternoon and were scheduled in hour time slots with twenty to twenty-five kids packed into each hour. Coaches would pin a paper number on your back and line you up: first, to get timed running around the bases; then to shortstop to field three grounders and throw to first; then to the outfield to field a few fly balls and make throws to home plate; and then into the dugout to put a helmet on and hit. Hitting was especially intense because a machine delivered the pitches, and you had only three swings, so you'd better put the ball in play, or at the very least, make good enough contact to hit a solid foul ball. Coaches stood along the base paths with clipboards and made notes next to your number, and if they liked something you did they would ask the person in charge for your name so they could have another look at your swing or your throw, so you'd get more reps, which was always a good sign. After that the coaches would instruct those eleven and twelve-year-old tryouts interested in pitching or catching to step to the side for a look, and that was it. They didn't ask the ten-year-old tryouts because a ten-year-old was not going to be a pitcher or catcher in that league his first year.

At the time it was common for coaches and managers to hold on to the same team for several years, so coaches and managers built reputations, and if they were perennial winners, of course, you wanted to make that elite team. For all of the coaches, ten-year-old boys were being drafted for the future and would typically be selected in the later rounds, so for the Pee-Wees coming up, coaches were basically looking for the best athletes that they could begin to shape themselves. I like to think that, as an athlete, the apple doesn't fall far from the tree, but I was Dave Garcia's Little Brother too, and he was on the Indians, so in a close call, that might work to my benefit. But these coaches were very competitive; they played to win, and how a kid felt did not factor into their decisions—being a legacy was not automatic. If a dad managed a team with one son, it was a courtesy to allow him to have the first shot at drafting his second son, but otherwise, brothers would sometimes be drafted by different teams and would compete against each other. My dad was not a coach, so the tryout was wide open and mine to win or lose. So I took the field, ran through the drills, and did my best, and after the tryout we all went home and waited for "The Call."

The tryout was held on a Saturday and afterwards we were told that we'd receive a call on Sunday or Monday from the coach who drafted us. The wait was nerve-racking, almost like a verdict being handed down by a jury, or worse, the decision being handed down by the judge; guilty, and you go to the minors, a huge disappointment, an irrational sense of failure even; or the majors, victory, and innocent of all mediocrity. That Sunday Dave had the decency not to torment me in church, and when we got home, I started pacing. Did we miss the call already? I went out to play for a while and came back to check again. And again. Finally, that night, the call came in. "Chris, this is Mr. Hite. I manage the Indians. Congratulations, you're on the team."

Our managers and coaches were, for the most part, Korean War veterans, like my dad, so they knew a little something about teamwork, structure, rules, and discipline. They were men, and sometimes they spoke to us like *we* were men.

I'll never forget Mr. Galley, one of our coaches. At our first practice of the season, after warmups, he gathered us together for an introductory speech. We huddled in a circle around him and took a knee, and after he introduced himself and our manager, we all told him our names. After dispensing with the formalities, he got more serious and proceeded to accuse us of having mothers who still nursed us. His precise language was a little more colorful than that, but we got the point. These guys weren't there to mess around, and personally, I found it highly motivational and very amusing. But the thing was, I appreciated what he said. Even at that age I understood it the way he meant it and I felt a little more mature for it. Sometimes it's okay for boys to be treated like men. I know it always worked for me.

I looked forward to baseball practice almost as much as I looked forward to games. During the first six weeks of the season we would practice five days a week after school leading up to Opening Day, and after that we played two games a week and practiced for three. Sitting in class I would stare out the window and into the sunshine, waiting for three o'clock to come, freedom, and then practice at five. There was a season or two where it seemed like we were getting afternoon showers between 3:00 and 5:00 almost every day. I hated those gathering clouds. I hated those showers. And I especially hated rainouts.

As I said, the Indians were a major league team and players ranged in age from ten to twelve, a range that kids no longer play in because the difference between a ten- and twelve-year-old in physical development is pretty significant. I realized this very early on in my ten-year-old season when I stepped into the batter's box in practice to face Bubba Stowe, our ace pitcher. Bubba Stowe was seven feet tall, and he had shoulders four feet wide. He was a pure, corn-fed country boy and when he brought his cheese, it was served *muy caliente!*

After making the majors my dad bought me my first bat. He let me pick it out myself and it was a beauty, a wood-grained Louisville Slugger. It was a perfectly balanced twenty-eight ounces of Thor's very thunder. It had Al Kaline's signature burned into it and even though I didn't know much about him, I sure liked his bat.

So I stepped into the box with Thor's hammer and looked up to see this tower wearing cleats and a cap go into his windup. One time, I read a writer's description of the experience a man had entering mortal combat. The man was so fearful that his bowels turned to water. It wasn't quite that bad, but I can say that my confidence in this encounter was not high. So Bubba brought his heat from the seventh floor and buried it in the catcher's mitt, the sizzle of the seams cutting the air as it crossed the plate. I was like a four-and-a-half foot concrete statue. Our coach called out, strike one! I blinked back to life and as I stepped out of the box and rested the bat handle on my leg to check both of my jean's pockets for a defibrillator, I happened to look across the street at the fire station and took comfort that they had an ambulance there in case one of Bubba's pitches got away. We'd go there after practice to buy a soda from their machine and cool off from the heat, and one time I saw them return to the station with lights flashing and siren blaring, only to watch them pile out of the truck with Burger King bags in their hands. I just got served the cheese. Now I was ready to leave the batter's box and join them for the rest of the burger.

I stepped back into the box and faced off again against Bubba Stowe. I was ready this time. This time when his fastball thwacked the glove I flinched, so there was life there, a pulse. Progress. Strike two! Okay, so as I stepped out of the box again and reached down for some dirt to dry my hands, I realized that Bubba was not going to mess around with me. He would dispatch me with three pitches and not waste any more energy. I figured his next pitch would be another fastball in the vicinity of the first two, so I stepped back in, tapped the plate with the end of my bat, and got set. He wound up, threw, and I took my swing. There was the crack of the bat! And then, in my hands, was my cracked bat. I stood there frozen, staring at the fractured hammer, too stunned to move. But when I looked up, to my astonishment, the ball rolled weakly to his right and I took off for first, where I was thrown out easily.

I felt terrible about breaking that bat. I knew it wasn't my fault, but I felt bad for my Dad. Getting individual gifts was a rarity for us kids so even though I treasured that bat, I knew that he probably treasured getting it for me even more. I lost my bat in one swing that day, but as I rounded first base and ran back to pick it up, I had a sense that I'd gained something else in return.

Church

We went to church as a family every Sunday. One morning, as we were leaving the house before church, I found a tiny green tree frog on our front porch. It tried to hop away as I approached but I caught it and put it in my zippered pocket to save for after church. I didn't tell anybody I had a frog in my pocket during the ride to church but I was concerned about his well-being so I checked on my little friend about fifteen minutes into the service and saw that he was okay, but I couldn't let anyone see him so I quickly returned him to my pocket and, regretfully, didn't check on him for the next thirty minutes. This must have been before the advent of breathable cotton because when I reached for him as we filed out of church, I was very sad to find that he wasn't moving. I held him in the palm of my hand and poked his little legs but there was no life in him, so I found a bowl of water and dropped him in, but he wouldn't swim. There would be no Lazarus miracle on this Sunday, so I took him home and buried him. As I knelt there in the dirt, I couldn't figure out what I had done wrong, I couldn't pinpoint my transgression, but I knew the Church got him. Ultimately I knew that it was my fault, so I never tried anything like that again.

By the time I was maybe ten years old, after the Catholic Church moved away from conducting services in Latin, I pretty much had the English version of the liturgical celebration memorized, so I didn't pay much attention after they swung the smoke bomb at us early on, during the opening ceremonies. The best part of the service, for me anyway, was halftime. That would be after much standing and kneeling, singing words that would normally be spoken, a couple of readings, and then the Gospel account. After that, the congregation would settle in, and the priest would walk towards the front of the altar and tell a story for about ten minutes. If he was any good, he'd also toss in a few jokes. In the program it was called the homily, and if I had a favorite part about church, that would be it, but only if he was going to expound on the Gospel reading I'd just heard.

It wasn't until later in life that I realized that what I enjoyed hearing in those Gospels was the parables. The parable is and was a uniquely Rabbinic form of storytelling, one that unfolds the drama so that it can often be seen from three different perspectives, from that of the king, homeowner or father as one character, the son or servant as a second, and a third character as observer or actor. Somewhat similar to the fable, which uses animals as actors to inform children about moral right and wrong, the parable is a picture illustration that informs the listener about God's truth by setting the stage of everyday life as seen through His eyes. The stories were usually presented with an unexpected plot twist towards the end that had to be caught, and that was what captured my interest. Jesus was an itinerant Jewish rabbi, and a master of the parable. But Alexander the Great preceded Jesus by three hundred years and through his conquests, spread the Greek language throughout the known world, and with it, a more

Hellenized interpretation of parabolic teachings that eventually made its way into the Church. There was nothing intentionally wrong about those interpretations; they were just different, and they confused me when I was a kid because I could see and understand the Rabbinic message, so when the priest would wrap up his allegorical interpretation I always thought that I'd somehow missed the meaning. The priestly account was interesting, and I understood the interpretation, but I much preferred the original Rabbinic form of the story, which made more sense to me.

A Christian's suffering was something familiar to me because my older brother, Dave, used to enjoy tormenting me in church sometimes. On his best days, when messing with me wasn't enough, he'd go for the bonus of getting me in trouble. For those services where we didn't arrive early enough, the pews and extra fold-out chairs would fill up, so we'd have to stand somewhere along the perimeter. This gave Dave the opportunity to stand behind me, and during the most solemn moments, tap his knee at the back of my knee causing my knee to buckle. This was a problem for me because, while his indiscretion went undetected, after my knees buckled a few times I tried to push him back with my butt or move from side to side to avoid him but that only made me look like a poorly operated dancing puppet. Push-slide-buckle, push-slide-buckle. This was not a good look for me, and it was a potentially unhealthy development for the future of my tender hind parts. If he succeeded with a double legged tap I might even go down on both knees, which would spell certain doom for me.

One time his evil plan prevailed, and down on both knees I went. When it happened, my only recourse was to feign reverence, bow my head, fold my hands together, and pretend to pray, as if I accidentally missed one of the kneeling parts of the service. But I was well known to my family by then so I couldn't sell it, and they weren't buying. When that happened my mother shot me a look that I well understood. I was keen to her particular facial expressions, as I'd seen them many times before, and could read her so well that I knew, with the arch of an eyebrow or the purse of her lips, with which instrument she would choose to administer my punishment when we got home, and whether she would come at me left-handed or right-handed. If my face betrayed me and I inexplicably smiled, her countenance would become severe and her eyes would suddenly turn black, and a cold, sick fear would grip me. That was it. I was cooked. Advantage Dave.

When I got a little older my mother enrolled me in the Catholic version of a Bible study class. It was called CCE or CCD, I can't remember which and I never knew what those letters stood for. It seemed like more of a social gathering to me because the teacher was disinterested, the kids were always talking, and I never saw a Bible in that class. What I did know was that I did not want to be there—at all. It was held at the school where we went to church, which was in a different school district than mine, so guess what? I didn't know anybody at that party. So there I was, in a classroom, the last place in the world I ever wanted to be, especially at night, with a roomful of strangers who had no interest in getting to know the kid from the other school. Such fond memories . . .

A year later a buddy of mine from my baseball team was sentenced to the same evening fate. Our parents or my older sisters took turns driving us, so after getting dropped off, we'd wait for the taillights to disappear and then we'd walk down to the Kmart a few blocks away and mess around in the toy department until it was time to go back. Apparently roll was never called because we never got caught.

My mother was a staunch Catholic and her intentions were good, but some of the privileges my parents provided for us, and more specifically, anything that had the word "lesson" attached to it, were wasted on me. Unfortunately that was before there was such things as private coaches in baseball. It was before anyone ever imagined that a boy who loved baseball could get individual hitting and pitching lessons. I would have arrived early and stayed late for something like that.

The best time of the church year was the church bazaar. I think it was sponsored by Budweiser. Well, they had a Budweiser truck out there every year anyway. And by the time we got there the priest was more jovial than usual. He also had a slightly red nose. It was good to see him happy and having fun.

The bazaar started in the early afternoon and lasted into the night. There would be barbecue, a variety of drinks, a cake walk, a dunking booth, and all sorts of other games to be played. Kids would be running everywhere as parents gathered around the roulette wheel and played other adult games. It seemed like the whole congregation would turn out; it was so packed with people as we all celebrated and eventually waited for the ultimate prize, a raffle for a car at night. I remember one cake walk game I was involved in. The number I was standing on was called out and I went to the booth to collect my prize, a bottle of Johnny Walker red label and a bottle of Johnny Walker black label. I was twelve years old. And they let me take both bottles with me with no questions asked. Thank you, Jesus! I don't know how I got them home undetected, but I hid them in my closet for a couple of years. I opened one eventually and took a sip but it didn't taste good, so I turned them over to my parent's liquor cabinet and never told them about it. Apparently I wasn't ready for the cowboy life I saw in the movies just yet.

My parents weren't drinkers, so those bottles stayed in their cabinet for years. I eventually sampled them some years later and after a few rounds I reckoned that maybe a cowboy could get something out of church after all.

Big Girls & Little Girls

I have three older sisters and two younger ones. In our house we referred to the three older ones as The Big Girls and the two younger ones as The Little Girls. My two brothers and I were The Boys.

I knew as much about my little sisters growing up as I did my older sisters, which is to say, I didn't know much about them at all. I wasn't paying attention; I was lost in my own world, and they did girl stuff, which didn't hold a lot of interest for me. If anything, they were more of a curiosity.

I remember one day when we were still living in Kansas City. My mom sent me down to the grocery store to buy some milk and bread. We lived on State Line, named so because we lived on the street that bordered Kansas City, Missouri, from Kansas City, Kansas. We lived on the Missouri side. I guess it was a somewhat busy street with the bank at the top of the hill on one end and the grocery store down the hill on the other end. So I walked down the hill to the grocery store to get a few things for my mom. I was five years old.

While at the store I stole a pack of gum. I don't recall the actual act of thievery, but I do remember coming home and sharing my loot on the side of the house with my sister Sharon, who promptly turned me over to the authorities. (That would be Mom and Dad.) I'm sure I was sent to bed without dinner and probably spanked and grounded for my transgression, but I don't have a memory of that. The memory I have is of my mother marching me back down the street to the grocery store to confess my crime to the store manager, return what remained of his stolen merchandise, and to apologize. Standing in front of that man was embarrassing to say the least, and I was properly ashamed. I think I even cried. But my mother was teaching me a valuable lesson, and it was a hard lesson learned for me, one that was bitterly received. Standing before that man I got the message loud and clear: I should never share anything with Sharon again.

But that was the role of my little sisters. They were the informers, and they set up an alliance, or cabal, of like-minded girls in the neighborhood to establish law and order, not for them but for us boys. Then by some secret decree, they expanded their powers of law enforcement to include all the boys of our ages who lived on our block. On our nation's currency it is written, "e pluribus unum." On their charter it was written, "I'm gonna tell on you."

When The Little Girls weren't patrolling our activities, they engaged in some of their own. They played four square and hopscotch, which they considered very serious business; they climbed trees; they rode bikes; they played games in which they had to run; and they were masters at jump rope, as in two jump ropes going at one time, what I later learned was called double

Dutch. For that, one girl on either end held two ropes, one in each hand, and circled them in opposite directions, so that, while one rope was hitting the ground, the other was at the apex of the circle. While two twirled, one or more girls would time the ropes and jump in. It was a very cool game to watch, and they were good at it. While indoors, they loved to play with their Barbie and Ken dolls. They didn't really know what boys or dads did, so Ken always went to work. But that playtime for them was magical. They probably did other stuff, but like I said, I wasn't really paying attention. I do remember that they loved Bobby Sherman, The Osmond Brothers, and The Jackson 5. They spun those records all the time. My youngest sister, Lisa, was absolutely devoted to Donny Osmond and was convinced that she was going to marry him one day.

The Big Girls didn't care for us too much because they had to babysit us younger siblings as soon as we started popping out. Apparently watching after us was not an altogether pleasant experience for them, though I know not why.

I didn't spend a lot of time with my older sisters, but I do have some pretty fond memories of them. One of the things that teenage girls liked to do back in the late sixties was dance. I don't know if teenage girls still do this, but my sisters used to have their friends come over to talk, to listen to records for hours, and dance. Between the three of them, and Mom's record contribution, they had an enormous collection of LPs and 45s that ended up having a huge influence on my own musical preferences. It was pop, it was rock, and it was Motown. It was The Beach Boys, The Who, The Spinners, Bill Withers, Crosby, Stills & Nash, Bob Dylan, Seals & Crofts, Blood, Sweat & Tears, Chicago, Al Green, and Stevie

Wonder, and songs like "California Dreamin'," "Reelin' in the Years," or "Cracklin' Rosie." But not all of them were upbeat. I remember spinning some of their records when I was alone, like McCartney's "Uncle Albert," The Beach Boys' "In My Room," the Carpenters' "We've Only Just Begun," and Glen Campbell's "Wichita Lineman," which had a big impact:

I hear you singing in the wire,
I can hear you through the whine...

and the crusher line,

And I need you more than want you,
And I want you for all time,
And the Wichita lineman,
Is still on the line.

I may not have understood exactly what he was saying, but it sounded like a cowboy song to me. Somehow even a young boy knew that guy.

It was a normal thing for me to walk into the house and hear music playing in the living room or to see six or more girls in shorts and bare feet just grooving and dancing away to Mitch Ryder & The Detroit Wheels. I don't think they ever noticed me, but I would just stand there and watch them because their actions were so foreign to me that I couldn't comprehend what they were doing. To me they may as well have been aliens from another planet, but from a galaxy with really good music. So I would stand there staring at them, and even though I couldn't figure it out then, when I look back now, I realize what I was seeing was pure elation. They were together and they were bonding and they were happy just to dance. Their dancing was pure and innocent, a picture of freedom and joy. They looked like the happiest people I'd ever seen.

My sisters had so many friends. Just on our street alone they had four or five of them, so there could be as many as eight girls dancing at one time! One of their friends was Brenda; I'll never forget Brenda. She was a raven-haired beauty, and my first crush. My first girlfriend was a curly haired redhead back in Kansas City named Judy. We used to sit in the back of the bus on the way home from kindergarten where I would give her "Hollywood kisses." But alas, I had to leave her behind when we moved to Texas. Parting was such sweet sor—

Anyway, Brenda was different. I was eight now, more mature, and Brenda was a *woman*.

When the girls were outside, I remember they would sometimes play a ring toss game that I never saw played anywhere else. The game was played in the street, like volleyball or badminton (or as we called it, badmitten), except in this game there was no net. A seam in the street divided the two sides where four to six girls played as teams. The ring was red, ridged, and made of a firm tubular rubber (like a garden hose), maybe eight inches across with the tube around two inches in diameter. The server would stand in the back corner, like in volleyball or tennis, and toss the ring using whatever kind of spin or wobble she could fashion, making the catch as difficult as possible while trying to place it where her opponents weren't. If an opponent successfully caught the ring, it would have to be returned using the same hand with which it was caught, and the ring would be volleyed back and forth in that way until it was dropped. The game was played to a score of 21, and the girls would play competitively, in bare feet wearing shorts and t-shirts, or maybe even halter tops. It was intense to watch, and if Brenda was around I'd stick around to watch them play. And when Brenda sat out and watched from the sidewalk, I'd occasionally put a lizard down the back of her shirt as a token of my love. I was smooth like that, even at an early age.

So the game would go on: leads were captured and lost, sides changed, and after awhile dusk would settle in and the sun would go down. The girls would eventually retreat together and maybe meet up with some of the neighborhood boys to sit in a circle on a driveway and play guitars and sing and talk into the night. But again, they just always seemed joyful.

I later learned that that game was called deck tennis, a game that originated on a ship's deck and played back as early as the 1930s and 40s. It was played with a net, but in their street game the net was imaginary.

The music my sisters brought into our home lives on in my collection today, but eventually that ring toss game faded into the mists of our history, like the pet rock, soap-on-a-rope, and the neighborhood milkman. And into that mist Brenda vanished as well, married, suddenly, to our neighborhood milkman! Gone from Carvel forever. The milkman! Son of a—!

And the Wichita lineman,
Is still on the line…

The Boys

For most of my childhood I pretty much lived in the shadow of my older brother, Dave. He was a good athlete and popular with the girls, even at an early age, so my name, until he left high school, was Dave Garcia's Little Brother. My younger brother, Landry, was a cute kid growing up, but of the three of us, Dave definitely got the looks. He wouldn't allow me to hang out with him much, but I got the impression that he was a pretty cool guy.

Dave was an artist at an early age. Even his doodles were good. Unfortunately, even though both Mom and Dad had that artistic gene, art was not really encouraged in our house as a profession, so he never fully developed his skill. But he did take art lessons, and his art was good. In his teenage years he'd draw beautiful murals on entire walls of his bedroom, and he painted pictures for my mom and sisters that still hang framed in their homes today.

Dave's neighborhood friends were Bob's older brother, Bill, and Jay Tucker, a kid that lived next door to my beloved Brenda. Jay had an older sister who hung out with my older sisters and an older brother named Stan, who was the neighborhood Adonis. Dave was a year younger than Bill and Jay, and they weren't in the same grade level at school, so Dave always had other friends who came to our house, but they lived further away. Whenever there was a game to be played in our neighborhood, it was always Dave, Bill, and Jay against me, Bob, Kelly from midway down our block, Jimmy, who lived at the end of the block, and whatever other victims we could round up. It didn't matter how many guys Bob and I had on our team, we lost every single game we ever played against those three older guys.

Landry was the baby of the family, and a very cute kid. We nicknamed him SRK for Spoiled Rotten Kid, mostly because the women in our family doted on him. But that wasn't his fault. He was young and needed the additional attention. And honestly, if anything, as he got older, he got less and less attention, until the kid was practically on his own.

With each kid, supervision and attention, and even photographs, seemed to dwindle. There were shoeboxes full of photos of my three older sisters. But by the time they got to me, there were only six torn or folded photos in a cigar box, and those got pinned to bicycle spokes to make noise. By the time we got to Landry, he was having to fend for himself, teaching himself how to cook as soon as he could look over the stove top, about age five, just to survive. He was so small that he would stand in front of the stove scrambling eggs and flipping pancakes with his hands doing the work above his head. He was a resilient kid with the metabolism of a rabbit, which meant he was hungry all the time, so by the age of seven, he was cooking full meals for himself.

Landry was a tinkerer. He liked to figure out how things worked, so he was always taking things apart and putting them back together again. One time he took a clock apart and reassembled it to run backwards. He got that skill from our dad. Dad could repair just about anything, and he could build things without schematics or directions—he once built a doghouse from a picture in his brain. When we were living in Kansas City, Dad converted our garage to a bedroom for his mother. Those are the things that Landry got from Dad. He was like a little Ben Franklin.

So, being in the middle of these two talented and good-looking brothers of mine, and being a middle child in the family, I guess I was sometimes looking for attention. I may have even had a reputation in our family for stirring things up on occasion. At least that's the rumor. Unfortunately, I didn't always think things through and wasn't always smart in the way I acted out. Being the middle brother, I would sometimes pick on my little brother. He was five years younger than I, so I had to wait until he aged enough to get picked on. But when he was finally ripe, I was ready. I didn't really hurt him in a way that made him cry. Sometimes I'd just punch him in the arm if he was passing by. Other times, if I was walking behind him, I'd trip him. This I learned from Bob's brother, Bill. Other times I'd drop him on the ground and sit on his stomach with my knees pinning his arms to thump his chest until he started yelling. This is how a middle child seeks attention. And this is how I made my older brother appear.

Anytime I picked on Landry, Dave would intervene, usually by picking me up and tossing me on the ground. And that's all he'd do, just lift me up, chunk me in the dirt, and walk away. But apparently I was seeking his attention all along because then I'd start picking on *him*. This is not what a smart person does, and these were the types of behavior patterns that allowed my mother to eventually sum me up so easily. As Dave would walk away I'd poke him in the back to remind him that he had not been excused yet. If he kept walking, I'd start taunting him by calling him names, like yellow, or worse, a yellow-bellied sap sucker, which always got things going in a cowboy movie, and other words I'd learned that, when projected at a volume within my mom's hearing, would land a bar of soap in my mouth, and she wouldn't even bother using a fresh one.

At some point he'd have enough of me and turn around. This was when the reality of my stupidity came into clear focus. No time to waste now. It was time to RUN! That's when Dave would chase after me. I always thought that I was faster than I actually was because for some reason, I always thought I could outrun him, or put a move on him and juke him off his feet. I'm telling you, I was not a very bright kid. I could elude him for awhile but he always caught up, and then he'd pin me on the ground the same way I'd pinned Landry, giving me a dose of my own medicine. One time, when I actually got mad at him and lost my temper, he dropped a tire around me, pinning my arms at my sides and just leaving me there to cool off. But my brothers and I had an unwritten rule: we never punched each other in the face or body. Punches were only directed at the arms, and we called them pokes. I never actually fought with Landry, and when Dave and I did fight, we only wrestled, and I always lost.

While Dave was the ladies' man, Landry was born with an old soul. When he was very young, at dinner time, he would always fall asleep in his highchair. We'd look over and see him face planted in his empty dish, so Mom or one of the Big Girls would clean him up and put him to bed. By the time he was five years old he was putting himself to bed. We'd be eating dinner and suddenly discover that he wasn't at the table anymore so we'd have to go looking for him. And that's where we'd find him, fast asleep in his bed and out for the night. He was like the perfect kid!

However, being the baby of the family, adorable as you might be, sometimes had its disadvantages, especially if you had two older brothers. Dave was a cool guy, but sometimes I could get him involved in my little schemes.

One night, while Landry was sleeping, Dave and I took our tape recorder to another room and recorded a bomb dropping sound effect, which consisted of a high-pitched whistling sound descending in pitch until we made our explosion sound. We recorded that a few times and played it back until we thought we had it right. Then we'd go back into our bedroom with the volume turned up full blast and play that in Landry's sleeping ear. It was mean, I know, but it had the desired effect as he rose up yelling at us and calling us farts, except he hadn't perfected his *r*s yet so it came out, "Fawt!" Then he'd put his head back on the pillow and say, "Sssick!" which was an abbreviation for, "You make me sick!" These were two of Landry's patented expressions, and the exact responses we were looking for!

I didn't mind being called Dave Garcia's Little Brother growing up because in reality, I looked up to him. He never beat me up like other older brothers did and he never treated me badly so the truth was, I liked him. And Landry? He was a great kid and I do regret the way I treated him sometimes. You couldn't help but like him. We all had our separate lives of mischief, but we never got into any real trouble, and as brothers, we always had each other's backs, and we always kept it tight.

The Locust Hunt

When we didn't have enough guys to get a game going at the ballpark, we'd play a smaller game in the street, or we'd play home run derby, or hot box in our yard between houses. But we had extracurricular activities as well, like lawn darts, ping-pong, or our summer long game of hunting cicadas. We called them locusts, and we kept a running count.

The two most favored weapons in our neighborhood were the rubber band gun, and the slingshot. The slingshot was a simple Y-shaped plastic and metal piece with two thick rubber bands or tubes extending from the tops of the "Y" and connected six inches down on either side to a small leather pouch. At some point people would call them wrist rockets, but we called them slingshots.

There are periodical species of cicadas, some that emerge every thirteen years, and some that arrive every seventeen years, with different shapes and coloration, but ours was the green, annual "dog day" cicada that shows up every summer. One of the great sounds of summertime was listening to that first male start his mating call, with the other males joining in until it became this symphony song, rising in volume into a pitched buzzing crescendo, and then the sound would ease as they took a breath and cleared their throats, and then the cacophony would begin again. Undulations of that droning song served as the background music of our summer evenings.

Cicadas are the loudest insect on the planet, and there were millions of them in our neighborhood. I don't know how the game originated, but put a slingshot in a young boy's hands and something is headed for the endangered species list, and that is precisely what we did to those locusts, at least on our block anyway.

In our neighborhood we had kids of all ages, from five years old to eighteen years old, and we were always outside, day and night. All of us could hop a fence at a dead run, knowing exactly where to toe a chain-link fence or find the footing of a wooden one. We climbed high into trees, we jumped off of rooftops, and we knew how to land and roll when we fell or got knocked down. And we really knew how to handle a slingshot.

The key to hitting a target with a slingshot is finding the right rock. Not too big and not too small, the more rounded, the better. So before we went on the hunt, we gathered rocks from the street, from the sidewalk, and from neighborhood yards. And when I say we, I meant my little sisters. They played a part in these games, too. They were the gatherers and we were the hunters. When we ran out of rocks we used chinaberries, but they were usually too big and that milky stuff from the stems was sticky and would gunk up the pouch. So the perfect sized rock would be bigger than a pea, but smaller than a chinaberry. Once we had a pocketful of rocks we would begin, and the game was simple. Whoever had the biggest pile of locusts at the end of the summer won.

Tracking locusts is not easy. While they may be abundant in numbers, their green coloring allows them to camouflage themselves very well in trees. When spooked, they either get quiet or fly away. So we would spread out, and the game would begin.

The first thing you do in a locust hunt is load your slingshot, and then you get real quiet and listen. The symphony usually started later in the day, closer to evening, but during the day you could hear the singular songs of individual locusts throughout the neighborhood. So you would locate the tree from which the sound came and walk slowly towards it. Because this was a regular activity for us, our hearing was very keen, and because we spent so much time outside, we were as close to being little Indians hunting buffalo as one could get, so our approach was stealthy. Once under the tree you would listen, locate, and look for the target's silhouette. Many times the locust would be sitting atop a branch, so looking upwards at a height of around fifteen to twenty feet, its body would be outlined darkly against the sky above. Sometimes we could hit it in one shot, but it usually didn't take more than three. Missing meant losing a good rock, and possibly spooking the locust away. We became so skilled that even though most of our rocks were not perfectly round and most of our shots would curve a little to the left or right, depending on how you positioned the rock in the pouch, we were able to compensate for that and would play many of our shots on the curve, taking out our targets with relative ease. My brother Landry was too young for this game so one day during our hunt he and his friend Leroy captured a live locust, tied sewing thread around its body and flew it around like a kite. So while I was busy knocking them down, he's experimenting with putting them up. Again, Ben Franklin.

Because we were spread out for this game, and because not all participants in the game were completely trustworthy, my sisters and their friends felt the need to intervene, so they would follow us, and somehow they became self-appointed judges. They just naturally fell into it because, if there's one thing girls enjoy, beginning at an early age, it's keeping boys in line. At least one of them would follow each of us, like judges following a golfer, to ensure that the rules were being enforced. They also kept score and settled disputes by committee.

Sometimes the count would be disputed, usually by one of the older brothers who had a tendency to change the rules on the fly. And when I say one of the brothers, I meant one brother in particular who was skilled in the art of trickery and deception. To call him out would be indiscreet, or perhaps it would lack decorum, but his name began with a 'B' and ended with an 'L' and there were two letters in between. One day, he who shall remain nameless claimed to have one more kill than the committee accounted for. The game was stopped, and the ledger consulted. The committee was correct, their count was seventy-seven, his seventy-eight. He objected, they stood firm; he requested a sidebar, sidebar denied; he thundered, they reconvened and returned with the same count. Since it was my lead that he threatened, I cited *Plessy vs. Ferguson* and demanded a writ of habeas corpus. I was overruled. Eventually he deferred, claiming that counsel was elsewhere on urgent business. The matter resolved, we returned to our respective trees. Then the popsicle man turned the corner and the game ended.

Popsicle Man!

There was one event that trumped all other activities in our neighborhood. One singular manifestation that caused all games to stop. The event began with a series of notes off in the distance that when heard, was like gaining the sense of sound and hearing music for the very first time. It paralyzed us, stunned us, stopped us in our tracks. It was that siren song off on the horizon. What? It's in the neighborhood? It's heading this way! POPSICLE MAN!

You've never seen kids completely lose their minds like we did when the ice cream truck was headed our way. Games in progress would be halted immediately, and it was as if the world went into slow motion: a pitched ball would be in midair, but upon hearing that circus melody, in the twinkle of an eye, a batter in a street game would turn his head out of pure instinct and tilt his ear towards the sound—a reflex action that predates cave men —to instantaneously establish the truck's location, determine proximity, and calculate ETA. Math and physics were never so easy. In that moment the player would lose control of the use of his hands and release his bat as the ball conked off his head. Gloves would be dropped in the middle of the street; girls would crumple on the driveway, tangled in a heap as jump ropes were abandoned; hopscotch was halted as a hop was taken but the skip was skipped; soldiers abandoned their posts and jumped out of trees and treehouses; Barbie would leave Ken! And then the world regained its speed.

And so we ran in place, or in circles, or squares, until we could orient ourselves and reestablish motor skills, and then we scattered for our houses, shooting across our neighborhood like bottle rockets, screaming all the while, just in case anybody missed it: POPSICLE MAN! *POPSICLE MAN!*

In a frenzy, we flew home, flung doors open, and started turning things over in the house. We only needed loose change! Money! Need money! Where is it! We begged, we borrowed, we prayed. The sound was getting louder, the truck getting closer. Don't miss it! *DON'T MISS IT!*

Some people in other worlds called out, Ice Cream Man! But that wasn't us. We didn't have that kind of dough. We were nickel and dimers. We were getting popsicles! Then, wait—he's on our block!! He's headed this way!!! *POPSICLE MAN!*

He was an intimidating figure that popsicle man, all high up in that truck like he was the king of some kind of rolling ice cream palace. So when he leaned out of that window you had to be ready! The line was moving, and the palace engines were running! So there was the pressure to make a selection. What to get! Lime? Grape? An ice cream cup? *Ice cream cup?* What am I, a millionaire?

CARVEL DAZE

And then we'd be sitting on the curb after he pulled away, trying to take our time with our icy treats but having to eat quickly, as the melted juice rolled down our arms and dripped off of our elbows, all silent in the neighborhood except the drone of neighborhood locusts off in the distance, and the sweet slurping sounds of happy children.

Chris Garcia

Grandma Garcia

Grandma Garcia was a person like no one I've ever known before or since. Barely reaching five feet tall but stout with long white hair, she looked like a Native American woman in one of those sepia tone photographs from a different place and a different time, like one of those old photographs with torn brown edges, as if she walked out from some bygone era. Maybe that's because she was from Mexico. At a young age she was afflicted with arthritis, which left her with a slight hitch in her walk, but she was strong as sun-cured leather so that hitch never slowed her down. She was a unique character, and a tremendous, vibrant woman who loved her grandchildren mightily. But she was definitely not your prototypical grandmother. She was unpredictable and multidimensional, and in many ways she raised us kids, so while she kept us in line with her legendary flyswatter, she was also playful, funny, and sneaky. Oh yeah, and she loved Elvis Presley.

Because there were eight kids in the house, both my parents had to work just to clothe and feed all of us, and that left Grandma home during the day to corral their herd. I don't believe she was ever expected to cook or clean or look after us, but she was the type of woman who, when she saw something that needed to be done, just did it. I believe she did it out of love for her son, and out of a sense of duty to family, but I know she did it mostly out of love for us kids. I know that she loved me, and she always found a way to make me feel special.

Early every spring the mockingbirds would be up at dawn on the power lines that stretched across the rear fence line of our backyard, singing their morning song. Their song was "crees, crees, crees!" which was how my grandmother would pronounce my name: Crees! She would be at the kitchen sink washing dishes, looking out the window into the backyard and as the mockingbirds sang their song, I'd be walking through the dining room heading towards the refrigerator and she'd tell me, "Crees! They calling you!" She was always so good to me, and my biggest regret is that I never took the time to get to know her well.

Her family fled central Mexico during the Mexican Revolution, which was fought between 1910-1920. Bandidos and revolutionaries were on the loose and eventually the army occupied the house that her father built and took over the land they were living on. So my grandmother's family journeyed to the United States, moving to Detroit to look for work in the auto plants and eventually moving again to settle in Kansas City.

While in KC my grandmother worked wherever she could, from potato chip factories to laundromats. Brokenhearted from the loss of her first husband, she eventually married again and had a third son, my Uncle Charlie, but her second husband was a loser who left her on her own to raise her family. So together with her eldest son, she raised her five kids. To her great credit, all of her children managed to stay out of trouble and grew up to have good lives with large families of their own. A short time after my parents got married, she moved in with them.

An absolutely essential part of Grandma's day was watching her favorite soap operas, what she called her "stories." When Grandma was watching her stories, she was not to be disturbed. Her day would begin early, before any of us got up, to make breakfast for Mom and Dad, and send the meal in to them with one of my little sisters. Then, during the school year, she'd supervise as my sisters made lunches for themselves and us boys. I only found out later who was responsible for our peanut butter and honey sandwiches, where the honey would seep through the bread and crystalize by lunch time, giving the sandwich a little crunch. I don't know if that was my grandmother's idea, whether my sisters were sleep walking when they made them, or if we just ran out of jelly. The sandwiches weren't pretty, and nobody was trading their ice cream for them, but I thought they were delicious and they got the job done. I think that's why I now prefer my peanut butter with a little crunch.

After getting us off to school and Mom and Dad off to work, Grandma had the house to herself. First she'd clean, and then she'd begin prepping for dinner, or making her tortillas and beans. For that she'd mix her flour and water and whatever secret ingredients she used to make her tortilla dough and then she'd slap it around for awhile, separate it into little balls, about the size of a golf ball, and then shape them into little cupped patties. When she was finished she'd put them in a clay bowl with a cloth cover to sit for a few hours until the dough fully rose. Then she'd go into her room to watch her stories.

She had two favorite chairs: her rocking chair, which was in the house, and her foldout lawn chair, the kind with a metal frame and green and white interwoven textile webbing, which she kept in the garage. I have a vision etched in my brain of her sitting on those chairs, feet crossed at the ankles, knitting or crocheting something new, or sewing something old. But I mostly remember her sitting on that lawn chair in the garage while the doors were open, with our dog tied up next to her, lying sleepily at her feet as she looked out and enjoyed her day. She worked that garage, cleaning it and doing laundry and taking occasional breaks to sit and sip on a cup of coffee. In the afternoons after school she'd even be out there in her chair rolling newspapers on her lap, helping out my brother Dave and me with our route. And she was faster at rolling than we were! Of course, we never appreciated it back then but really, whose grandmother does that? Who does that, period?

While my mother favored the spatula, my grandmother's disciplinary weapon of choice was the flyswatter, and when she was sitting in one of her chairs, she held it across her lap at the ready, her hand on the wire handle like a gunslinger about to draw. When she did draw you had to make sure you were out of her range because she could cut the air with that thing like a Musketeer wielding a sword. It didn't matter if you were human, canine, or insect, if you were on her nerves, you were on her radar. And if you were on her radar, you were going to feel the sting, usually on the back of your leg, even if you were a fly. She was that good. And then, as if the sting wasn't enough, she would sometimes put an exclamation point on it. If I did something she didn't like she would make that sound of disgust or lost patience where the tongue skips off the ridge on the roof of your mouth, close to your teeth, "Tsz," followed by a contemptuous, "Granudo." As I whimpered away even our dog would look up at me like I was an idiot.

One of Grandma's favorite activities was going to Kmart. She pronounced it *K-Mark*. She looked forward to that outing and would even dress up for the occasion. She couldn't drive so at the end of every month she'd receive her Social Security check and ask my dad to take her. She always preferred company so sometimes she would ask me or one of my brothers to go with her. Each time, Dad would drop us off for an hour or two. It was always fun for us because we got to see her all dressed up, perfumed, and walking the aisles in the land of the blue light special. It was also cool because she would usually treat us to a little something, like a burger or a chocolate malt. Or she would share her bag of orange slices, her favorite candy. But she usually took my little sisters, Sharon and Lisa, for her K-Mark outings. They were pretty much her assistants, so I think that was her way of rewarding them, or saying thank you, or just spending time with her little girls.

She could also be surprisingly sneaky at times, like one of us kids. Sometimes she'd hear me in the hallway or in the bathroom and she'd pop her head just out of her doorway where I'd hear her say in a whisper, "Pssst! Crees! Come here!" When I got to her door she would motion me to come closer. "Go get me one of your mother's cigarettes!" This didn't happen often but I knew the drill so I'd liberate one from my mom's purse and take it to her. If no one else was around she'd invite me in, light it, and offer me a puff, which I always took, before turning me loose.

Grandma was also like a wizened elder, full of knowledge, which she was, and she had us convinced that she possessed incredible perceptive skills as well. On Christmas Day, when she was given a present to open we'd all watch as she accepted the gift, shook it gently, put it down on her lap to think for a moment, and then she'd guess what it was, unwrap it, and she was right every time. She was like Kreskin, or Grandma Carnac the Magnificent! Little did we know that earlier in the Christmas season, while we were still at school, she would pick through the pile of presents under the tree and open the ones with her name on them to see what she got, and then re-wrap them. She played that joke on us for years before we figured it out.

It was a real treat for all of us when Mom's mother came down for a visit and we could watch the two grandmothers interact. Mom's maiden name was Breting and our Grandma Breting was a hoot as well. She enjoyed her little nip of whiskey in the evening, maybe even two, if you insisted, and her favorite treat was candy corn. Her and Grandma Garcia's backgrounds couldn't have been any different, though. Grandma Breting and her husband were native born and had some financial success early on but took losses during the Great Depression, as most people did in this country and throughout the world. The two of them were socialites to some degree, hosting cocktail parties and enjoying some of the finer things in life, and they were able to remain on the right side of the tracks as the country dug itself out of that dark decade, after which my mom was born.

The two matriarchs were also different in the kitchen. While Grandma Garcia's specialty was cooking, Grandma Breting's specialty was baking and when the two of them were in the kitchen together it was magical. Grandma Garcia spoke English well but some of her words were a little broken. She pronounced Breting to sound like booty, so it was her and Grandma Booty commiserating in the kitchen, comparing notes and recipes and working like a team. They loved each other and acted like little girls at play when they were together. They were special, and we never ate so well as when the two of them were sharing the kitchen.

Without a doubt or debate, Grandma Garcia was the best cook in the neighborhood. Her fried chicken had no rival and her meatloaf no peer, but it was her Mexican food that really set her apart. We didn't have Mexican food restaurants on every corner of Houston the way we do now. But it didn't matter. Back then her cooking was better than anything a Mexican restaurant had to offer, and we had it practically every day. Anybody who ever ate one of her meals, especially her tortillas and beans, never forgot. And for that reason, it was normal to have our friends over for dinner. She always had something cooking and she loved to feed people. That wasn't just her love language, it was part of her being, and there simply wasn't a better cook in the neighborhood.

Charlie Brown

I've read that celestial objects orbiting anywhere near a black hole will gradually get pulled into its gravitational field and eventually sucked in, never to be seen again. Stars bigger than our sun routinely disappear into black holes, gone to infinity, in an instant. We had a dog named, Charlie Brown. His mouth was like a black hole.

I don't know how old I was when Charlie Brown came to our house. I don't remember who brought him home. But he was a pup when we got him, and after being handled by eight kids for a period of time, I suspect he became a little crazy. As a full grown dog he was a wild animal, and crazy mixed with wild animal is not a great combination in a family pet. You couldn't run with him in the backyard without having him nip at your heels, or flat out trip you. You sure as heck couldn't attempt scaling a fence without having him pull you down by your ankle. He was the ruler of our backyard, and he ruled absolutely. But his entire life was dedicated to escape.

We had a sliding glass door that led from our dining room into the backyard. Charlie used to stand on his hind legs and pound on that glass door with his front paws, just running in place, like he was attempting to gain traction and scale the house. I don't know if that's how he was telling us he was hungry or what, but he was usually mollified by food. And this is where the black hole comes into play. You see, Charlie Brown didn't eat his food, he inhaled it. And I mean that literally. Any food object that entered his gravitational field would get sucked in, never to be seen again. We used to toss him a slice of cheese, his mouth would open, and the cheese would be gone before his mouth closed. I never once saw him chew on his food. You could frisbee a slice of bologna in his general direction and he would suck it down, like a pneumatic tube, only faster.

Now, in order to feed him this way we had to crack open the sliding glass door just wide enough to get our arm through and toss him the food. It was the safest way without getting mauled, or losing a small appendage, or even a limb. But Charlie Brown was smart; he was an escape artist, and that crack was all he needed to stick his nose through, shoulder the door open, and muscle his way into the house. He was a strong dog, a midsized, chiseled brute. Part beagle, part retriever, and pure hellhound, I imagined him lifting weights out in the backyard, like a convict pumping iron and stacking time in solitary. Once he got a shoulder through there was no way we could stop him from entering so, once inside, if the front door was open, he was gone.

Once outside, Charlie Brown forgot his name. If you called, he wouldn't acknowledge. He was out, he was free, and he was going to do whatever he wanted, which meant sniffing things, peeing on things, and chasing cars. And when I say chasing cars, I mean attacking cars. He wouldn't just chase after them, he'd get his face out ahead of the front tire and try to bite it, growling all the while. God forbid that an innocent kid might happen to be riding his bike down the street while Charlie Brown was loose. Sorry kid, it was nice knowing you.

But the best of our Charlie Brown stories was the time when he broke through that small opening in the sliding glass door and charged towards the front door. When he got to the living room, however, the door was shut, and now he had screaming kids running him down so he spun around, in a panicked frenzy and headed back into the dining room, sprinting for his first visible escape route, the staircase. So he turned and clawed his way up the wooden staircase to gain the second floor, paws scratching and slipping on the tile floor landing as he scrambled and skidded furiously across the hall, into the upstairs bedroom, where he gained traction, bounced off the bed and leapt through an open window. What made that escape so memorable, outside of jumping out of a second-story window, which was a first for him, was the unique points of view of that leap. If you can, imagine being in that room to see a dog's hind legs disappear through an open window, or being in the room directly below it to see him drop, or on the ground across the street, raking leaves in your yard only to look up just in time to see a dog exiting a second-story window. . . . My sisters were in those rooms, and our neighbor was outside raking up his leaves at just the right time to see Charlie Brown take flight, only to hit the ground hard, like an attempt off a high dive gone horribly wrong. But Charlie Brown could take a hit. He staggered to the chinaberry tree and leaned against it, taking his standing eight count, and then he scampered off to do his thing. Our neighbor always looked at us a little sideways after that.

That fall did not kill Charlie Brown. It didn't even slow him down. The black hole, the backyard despot, the killer of cars—well, he died several years later, but he pretty much became a legend that day. He did have a good life with us, though. The garage was always open for him when he needed shelter from the weather or a break from the heat. And he did answer to one master, besides food, and that was Grandma Garcia. She loved him and cared for him, and because she could be firm and because she ruled her domain with a flyswatter, he obeyed her and loved her back. She would sit in her foldout chair at the edge the garage with him leashed and sitting at her feet as they both looked out into the neighborhood. It was the only time he was ever calm while tethered. They really belonged to each other.

I miss that crazy dog, and I always wondered what thought entered his mind when he crossed that window threshold that separated bedroom from open air, and he saw treetops for the very first time.

Mom and Dad

Twas The Night Before Christmas

Grandma Garcia & Charlie Brown

CARVEL DAZE

Big Girls & Little Girls

The Boys & Charlie Brown

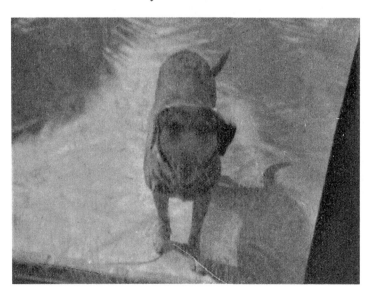

Can you guess which one is Buster Willis?

"Captain" Bob and me at Astroworld

The Indians

The Boys & Bob's brother Bill

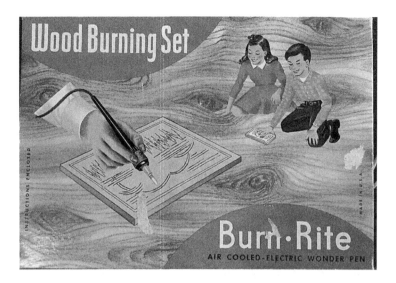

What could possibly go wrong?

Something's headed for the endangered species list!

The Crazy 8's!

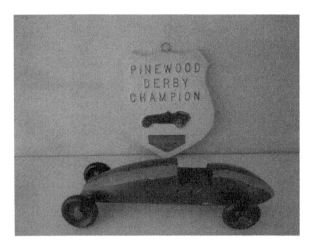

You can't beat Moog cars on race day!

CARVEL DAZE

The Paper Route

Dave and I had a paper route when we were young boys. I don't remember how long we had that route, but it doesn't seem like it was longer than two years? Maybe three? I do know that taking on the paper route wasn't my idea, nor was it my brother's. What kid goes out looking for work when he can spend all of his non-school time playing baseball and football? Not *this* kid, I can tell you that. I didn't even like chores. Heck, I hated making my bed in the morning. So how did two young, rowdy boys get roped into a paper route job without really knowing how it happened? Maybe, just maybe, it was Dad's idea. . . . But maybe he just made it *look* like it was our idea . . . Little did I know at the time that he was teaching us about responsibility and that this was part of his lesson plan for shaping his boys to become men.

Back then there were two newspapers in town: the *Houston Chronicle* and the *Houston Post*. We delivered the *Chronicle*. The *Chronicle* was delivered in the evenings on Monday through Friday, in the afternoon on Saturday, and in the morning on Sunday. One of my first memories of that process was the arrival of the newspapers, and how we wrapped them. We called it wrapping, but we were really rolling them. Back then there was a truck that dropped the wire-bound bundles at the end of the paperboy's driveway. The time of day depended on the day of the week. So Dave and I would move the papers inside the garage or just outside of the garage, depending on the weather and the season. It was our job to wrap them and deliver them during the week.

Keep in mind that I was maybe ten years old when we started. Dave would have been around twelve. Those bundles were heavy, and we had to pick them up and carry them up the driveway. Sometimes the bundles would arrive with a spool of string because, believe it or not, in the beginning we had to tie the papers with string before delivering them, and that wasn't easy for a kid with small hands. Let's review that high-tech industrial process for a moment, shall we?

There were certain days of the week we liked, and others we dreaded, because the papers contained more sections, which made them thicker and heavier on certain days than others. For instance, the best day for wrapping was Saturday, because the paper was small. The worst days were Wednesdays and Sundays. Wednesdays because of coupons and who knows what else they put in there, and Sundays because that was when they put shoppers and extra sections in the paper. So here was the process:

First, snapping off the wire. The bundles were bound with two wires by an over-zealous machine that did not want those bundles opened. Ever. It took its job very seriously. Those bundles would arrive so tightly bound that the wire would be cutting into the papers on the outside of the bundle. Jamming a pair of pliers or wire cutters into that wire required the sacrifice of at least one newspaper. That wire was thick, because things were strong back then, and it took two hands to snap it.

Next, the folding process. Kneeling on a concrete surface, we would place the paper in front of us with the open end closest to us and roll the paper up as tightly as we could. Then we would place the rolled paper upright between our knees and squeeze it in place as we took a piece of string and tied it in a knot around the paper. It was impossible for us to get a solid roll on a Wednesday or Sunday paper because the papers were bulky, so it was hard to get a good squeeze and tight roll on them. Eventually something called the rubber band was invented and we started using those. When finished we placed the rolled-up paper neatly in a pile on the floor to be loaded for delivery later. During the baseball season my sisters would help out with the rolling.

Dave and I had to deliver the papers by ourselves during the week, and most Saturdays. I'm guessing Dave made more deliveries than I did, but the idea was for us to take turns. We had a bike dedicated to the paper delivery job. The bike was big, long, and heavy. They still make them today except they're sold with tags such as "retro" or "old school." Back then it was like the station wagon of bikes. Our bike had these two large canvas saddle bags with a wooden frame attached to the back, where we loaded the papers. The idea was to cram as many papers into the bags as possible because we had a fairly long route, and we tried to make as few loading stops as possible. Wednesdays were a particular challenge to load because that's when the laws of science and physics intervened, which we hadn't covered in the fifth grade yet. Because the Wednesday papers were so big and heavy, if Dave and I overloaded the bags the bike would stand up on its back end, front tire in the air, like hi-ho Silver, away! Except we weren't heavy enough to counterbalance the weight and bring the front end back down. So we had to remove papers until we could mount up and establish balance, from the Latin, fulcrumus equilibriumus.

On rare occasions Dad would have time to help us on Saturdays but that was the easiest delivery day on the bike because the papers were small and we could tie them up tightly, like a relay baton. We could also get the entire route in one load. During the week we tried to toss the papers as close to a person's front door as possible, but on Saturdays we went for the porch. For that reason, on Saturdays we could work on our technique. You see, with the string- and rubber band-rolled newspaper there were basically three tosses you could use: the lob, where you put a high arc on your throw to land it on the porch with no bounce and minimal slide; the fastball, where you fire it at the front porch and bounce it off the bottom of the door; or the roll, where you threw it on a rope to purposely hit the ground low, maybe fifteen feet in front of the porch, so the paper could cartwheel end over end until it landed on the porch without hitting the door. Which throw to use depended on the location of the porch and whatever was in front of it. Dave and I were already baseball pitchers by then, so we were pretty good at hitting our spots. I don't think my Dad ever worried about either of us breaking a window. It never happened.

We made our collections once a month on weekday evenings. Dad would drive us to each house and wait in the street as Dave and I walked up and rang the doorbell. "Collecting for the *Chronicle*!" As I recall that scene now, I envision Dad as the mafia boss, sitting out in the car, smoking a cigarette, the warm glow of the ember lighting his face as his "boys" made his collections.

That brings me to the Sunday delivery. I have my fondest memories with Sunday deliveries because that's when Dad came with us. The papers were delivered to our house early in the morning, around 4:00. Sometimes I'd hear them drop but on most mornings I was sound asleep. My Dad could hear a light switch being turned on three houses down, so when those bundles hit the driveway he'd get up, make his coffee, and then wake us up. In the winter he'd make hot chocolate for Dave and me. I have no memory of wrapping or throwing papers on fair-weathered days, or even sweltering days. Maybe it's because we had no central air back then and we were acclimated differently. But I do remember those winter mornings. It was cold and dark outside, and the concrete was cold, but I was warm in my bed and Dad would wake me up so gently. I was always happy to see him, and I remember sometimes hugging him and telling him that I loved him. My dad was a tough guy, a Marine. His job kept him on the road on weekdays and he had eight kids, so he had little time for tender moments. But he was a sweet-hearted man and on those Sundays he was calm and quiet and easy with his boys. I remember a few times when I didn't get up; I didn't answer the call. When I did eventually get out of bed on those mornings I'd walk out to find just the two of them in the kitchen or dining room table after making the run. Neither one of them said an unkind word to me, and my Dad never tried to teach me a lesson about responsibility. I learned that in my own embarrassment and shame.

If we ever had conversations on those Sundays, I can't remember them, which is odd because it seems like I always pestered my big brother. And even though we were close in age, Dave never really picked on me. I picked on him. He might be patient for a minute or two, but if I persisted, he'd make the correction. Nobody ever accused me of being a bright kid. But there was none of that sibling rivalry on Sundays. I just remember wrapping the papers quietly, stacking them in the back of the station wagon, and sitting on the tailgate next to Dave as my Dad drove from one side of the street to the other, calling out the addresses from the list in his hand as we tossed those heavy papers onto the driveways. Occasionally we had to drop a paper onto a porch, so we'd have to hop out and run it to the door, but Dad kept the car rolling along so we'd have to run and catch back up. I remember we took our little brother, Landry, out on the Sunday run with us a couple of times. He was a little guy, maybe only five or six years old. On one of those cold mornings, he had his hands buried in his pockets and on that first run he fell out of the back of the wagon. We slowed down and eventually he did catch back up. He accused me of pushing him out, but to this day he has been unable to present any eyewitness testimony to corroborate his story. Shortly after that he was moved to the front seat, but he still tagged along for a few weeks until he somehow cracked the windshield with his head when Dad had to suddenly hit the brakes. Nobody wore seat belts back then—they were buried under the seats—and Landry was fine, but it was obvious that we brought him up too soon, so his paper route career ended abruptly after that. He had our respect, though. The kid was tough.

On a good day we'd finish just as the first light emerged—false dawn. On a bad day the papers were dropped late so we had to work late. If it rained we had to run them all to the front porch. That changed when Dave and I witnessed the greatest technological breakthrough in paper route history: the plastic bag.

The cap to our early Sunday morning run was another cup of hot chocolate. Dad would go back to bed, and Dave and I would watch bullfighting from Spain and then Paul Boesch's Houston wrestling with Mil (we called him Bill) Máscaras, Wahoo McDaniel, José Lothario, and Ernie Ladd. Our channel selections had increased from three to five options by then so if we were lucky we'd also get *The Three Stooges*. And yes, I said bullfighting from Spain.

Over those paper route years, I saw hundreds of front pages and headlines. It's interesting to me that the only ones I remember are those related to Watergate and the Vietnam War. And when I really look back on it now, I believe it may have been my Dad's paper route all along. I say that because I don't ever remember getting paid. Come to think about it, I never *did* get paid. Hey, wait just a minute here . . .!

Chris Garcia

Go Fly a Kite

"I went to my doctor and asked for something for persistent wind. He gave me a kite." —Les Dawson

On any given day, because we had so many kids living on just our block alone, there was activity all up and down the street, but mostly on our end. If you walked down our street you would inevitably step over at least three hopscotch boards, scratched onto the concrete by just the right type of rock, and there would be girls hopping and skipping on at least one of them at all times. At the same time, a handful of girls a little older would be playing jump rope in the adjacent driveway, and in the yard two houses down there would be a football game being played in the yard. Two houses down from that, young boys would be playing war games, which included climbing trees, jumping fences, and fighting off the enemy from a tree house. All the while the Big Girls might be sitting on the roof of a house down the block, talking to their girlfriends and some of the older boys that lived down the street. Some of them might have even been smoking cigarettes. But the one activity that brought us all together was flying a kite. I haven't seen one in the air for years and for the life of me I cannot figure out why.

Kites used to be popular and could be found displayed prominently in the front of any five-and-dime and in most grocery stores. The first ones I remember were made of thin paper, like wrapping paper, and framed in balsa wood. There were plastic ones that we eventually tried, but they were more expensive, so we made our first "paper or plastic" decision easily. Right next to the kites were balls of white string, but we didn't need that because we had a paper route and used a large spool of string to roll the papers, so we always had plenty of string. Lastly you needed a handle on which to roll up and hold the string. We always had a foot-long piece of broom handle for that, but you had to make sure you securely taped down that first part of the string to the handle; otherwise, if you weren't paying attention, the string would run out and that kite would sail away.

Flying a kite required the assistance of our older sisters because somebody needed to fashion a tail for the kite, usually made out of a cloth strip of an old sheet and tied to the end. It also required somebody to teach us how to launch, so once things got going, it wasn't unusual to have four or five kites in the air simultaneously. The key at that point was to stay far enough away from each other that our lines didn't cross, which usually brought our aircraft crashing down, sometimes in the street. Those soldiers didn't always survive. Whether they crashed into the street, tore into our trees, or dive-bombed into a yard, the kites usually needed some form of tape related triage to get back into the air. The worst was when lines would cross and the string would snap and the kite would set sail for streets or neighborhoods unknown. When that happened, anyone not flying the bird would hop on their bikes and race out to follow it, sometimes for blocks, until it was found. Other times it would outrun us, and we would just sit there on our bikes in the middle of the street and watch it soar away until it disappeared. I remember the heartbreak of losing a kite one time as I watched it depart from me, long gone. I would just stare off into the distance until I heard the crash and saw the plume of smoke over the distant tree line. Man down . . . we lost him.

Even some adults would get involved when we started our aerial assault on the sky. There was a young man and wife who lived across the street from us, named Mr. and Mrs. Saul, and they had two small blond-headed kids who were too young to play with us. The Sauls were friendly, and I don't remember much about them except Mr. Saul shot a nail into his leg while mowing his front lawn one time, so that was pretty cool. I think my dad took him to the hospital. But I also remember that Mr. Saul was the king of the kites. I'll never forget the time he put one into the air. He didn't use string, he was a fisherman and used fishing line on a spool, so his line was not going to get cut and he was not going to lose his kite.

I don't know where he got his kite from. He just showed up outside with it late one afternoon and put it up. And he didn't need anyone's assistance throwing it into the air while he ran down the block either. He just let out some line and lofted it up himself, and it held. He obviously understood the winds the way we understood . . . well, we were kids, so we pretty much didn't understand anything. We all watched as he let out more line and more line until the kite really caught the wind and his spool started spinning. Up and up it went, darting this way and that, but never too far one way or another, because he would tug down left, and then right, and the kite would correct itself and fly properly.

He put that kite up so high that it became nothing but a dot in the sky. You had to really focus to see it. And then he tied his line to his tree and left it there for us to watch. So we watched it, and sometimes someone lost it so we'd have to help them get sight of it again. And then the light faded, the sun went down, and it was dark, and he just left it there, flying all night.

The next day the neighborhood woke up early to see if that kite was flying, and sure enough, there it was, just a stationary speck in the sky, flying high with the birds of the air. He left it up for a couple of days, and we marveled at it in between the games we played. And then one morning it was gone, shot down or caught in the propeller of some passing plane. That kite was gone forever, and to my surprise Mr. Saul didn't seem too upset about it. He just smiled at the solemn assembly gathered in the street outside his yard and walked inside his house. That night I went to bed thinking about Mr. Saul and his kite so high in the sky. Man, he really knew how to let 'er fly.

So, is there a message to this story? Well, yeah. That should be obvious, man. Do yourself a favor and go fly a kite!

Chris Garcia

Danger, Will Robinson!

Parents today would be locked up and sent away if they allowed their children to play with the toys we played with when we were kids.

I looked up lawn darts online recently and saw the version of what's being played today—these little plastic shafts with weighted, bulbous plastic ends that, when thrown, might fall ever so gently and safely into or around the plastic circle that was their target. That's very nice. Harmless. If you happened to be accidentally hit by one of those you might think that someone had thrown a giant marshmallow at you.

Our lawn darts had metal shafts, maybe 12" to 18" long with red or blue flights (hard plastic feathers) and tipped on the business end with an actual silver steel point. Medieval archers would have been envious. The traditional way to play is to put two plastic circles, roughly the size of a Hula-Hoop, on either end of the yard, line up players on one end, and have them lob the darts underhanded into the circle at the other end. That made the game too slow for us, so we lined up with players on each end and played the game that way, by throwing the darts towards each other. Left to their own devices, kids often change the rules or make intelligent decisions like that. But soon that game got boring, so we decided to put one hoop in the front yard and the other in the back, with teams in both yards, and throw the darts over the house. Of course, that added a new wrinkle to the game, Dodge Death. Finally, something worth playing.

Another toy that we were allowed to play with was a wood-burning kit with a Wood Burning Wonder Pen, *"For boys and girls from 7-16 and up!"* Here was a good idea for kids. A kit with a large pen, roughly the size of a magic marker or highlighter, with a metal end that heated up and burned into wood when plugged in. The wood actually smoked. How could anything possibly go wrong with that?

My older sister had a chemistry set, obviously designed by someone who hated children. Among other things, the set contained small, clear plastic canisters with brightly colored chemicals that looked exactly like crushed rock candy. It had to be delicious! So I ate it! I'm told I was rushed immediately to the hospital to have my stomach pumped, but I have no recollection of that.

My younger sisters had an Easy-Bake Oven, a revolutionary role-playing device for young girls. To me, that thing was like magic because suddenly, with little or no training that I saw, my sisters could bake. And they were good at it! Those little tin pan cakes they made were delicious! Any time they gathered their friends and pulled that oven out they were like neighborhood celebrities. Every boy up and down the block would try to get in on the treats, including me. The genius mechanism at play for that little death trap was a light bulb that may have been a miniature version of the lights you might find at a professional football stadium. I got impatient one time and reached in for my cake without permission and accidentally touched that bulb with my hand. When I jerked my hand back I was pretty sure the skin missing from the back of it was still on that bulb. Have you ever caught the smell of burning flesh? It might be good with a little mustard, or perhaps paired with a perky chardonnay.

And finally, there were the clackers, two tempered glass balls, slightly larger than a golf ball, knotted at the ends of two thick cords or string that were attached to a key ring in between. The idea was to hold the keyring with your thumb and forefinger and sort of bounce your hand up and down to get the two balls clacking together and then to get them swinging out wider and wider until you could rapidly move your hand up and down as the balls swung like wings beating, clacking at the top and bottom of their flapping swing. The longer you kept those balls clacking, the better you were. If you missed your opportunity and the balls didn't come together, or when the balls got out of alignment, they would swing out wildly and bash your forearms, sometimes right on the bone, always the best spot.

News reports started coming in about those glass balls shattering and blinding kids so the makers switched to plastic. We never heard of that happening to anyone we knew so we treated the news like a rumor and swung away. But you could always spot a clacker kid at school because, if they weren't walking with a dog and a stick, their arms were usually colored red, purple, and yellow below the elbow.

Buster Willis and The Jump

Next door to us, on our left side, lived the Willises. It was Mr. and Mrs. Willis and their two boys, Buster and Jeffery. Buster was about a year and a half younger than me, and his little brother was a couple of years younger than him.

The day we moved into our house I was sitting with my new friend, Bob, on our front porch. Our friendship was about thirty minutes old. As we sat there poking sticks in the dirt we watched as the Willises' green, wood-paneled station wagon crossed the street in front of my house and pulled into their driveway. As soon as that car came to a stop, the back door flew open and a pudgy little kid dressed in a full purple costume raced across my front yard, arms extended in front of him like he was flying, singing, "Nah-nah-nah-nah-nah-nah-nah-nah-nah . . . Batman!" I don't know what that kid was thinking but Bob and I looked at each other and agreed without speaking. It wouldn't be the last time we roughed up little Buster Willis.

Buster Willis was a momma's boy. His mother ruled that house next door and seemed angry most of the time, maybe because she was raising a little monster but more likely because her husband's business dealings had taken a hit and they had to move into a neighborhood that was beneath her. We may have enjoyed playing with Buster boy if he hadn't been such a spoiled kid. We did try to include him in our games, but it became evident early on that he couldn't handle our style of play, which was ruled by the laws of the jungle. In order for us to get a game going in the neighborhood, guys like Bob and me had to gather our friends together to team up against our older brothers and their friends. We usually outnumbered them, but that didn't matter. We were always doomed from the start, and they would show us no mercy. They played hard, they wrestled hard, and they tackled hard. Bill Layton, Bob's older brother, was the leader of those brutes. He was the fastest kid on the block, the most athletic, and the most vicious. He'd throw a body block tackle at you to intentionally land you on the sidewalk; he'd run you down from behind and shove you into a tree while you were running with a football at full speed; or he'd toss you into a bush full of thorns. And then it would be fourth down. Buster Willis couldn't hang with that, and he revealed his true self to us early on. His signature move when he got hurt was to throw his fists down, stomp his feet, and quit, remaining silent as he stormed back to his house, but wailing out loud as soon as he hit the garage so his mom could hear him cry. There were times when she would come out and holler at us, but she never saw what we saw so we didn't pay much attention to her. She may as well have been screaming at Vince Lombardi's defense anyway.

The classic Buster Willis story, though, was when he attempted to make The Jump. Back around that time there was a motorcycle daredevil named Evel Knievel, who jumped his motorcycle from one giant ramp to another, crossing over anything from a multitude of busses or cars to even the Snake River Canyon. In

1968 he jumped over the Caesar's Palace fountain but crashed into the landing ramp, fracturing multiple bones in his body and suffering a concussion. He was a legend.

Well, as kids, we'd set up a ramp on a sidewalk using a 4 x 8 piece of plywood as the ramp, with a base built beneath it and two-by-fours supporting it from the top of the ramp, angled in the opposite direction back down to the ground, so that it looked a little like a leaning A-frame, long on the ramp side and steeper but shorter on the support side. It was about three feet high at the launch point. We didn't have enough materials for a landing ramp, so we landed our bicycles on the ground. To make the game interesting, kids would lie down, side by side, at the end of the ramp so we could see how many kids we could jump. Clearing five or six kids was pretty easy so after running out of kid bodies we'd set up cardboard boxes to extend the distance.

This particular day we had our ramp set up on the sidewalk across the street from Mr. Ruhl's house. Mr. Ruhl was a Ford man: he loved his car and every other day he was out in his driveway sitting on a plastic bucket, washing or polishing his baby in flip-flops and shorts. Ex-Navy, he was always tanned and still in great shape, but he had a look in his eyes that was a little unnerving. Most of the dads in our neighborhood were ex-military so they all had that same type of look. You didn't talk back to men like them and nobody today would attempt to stare those men down. He didn't talk to us kids much but he was an adult so that was normal. He did smile on occasion and his daughter was my age and a frequent playmate of my younger sisters, so he was at least familiar to us. Anyway, after several of us made successful jumps, it was Buster's turn.

There were no practice runs when jumping ramps. The idea was to get your bike moving as fast as you could by the time you hit the ramp so that you could clear a respectable distance. We must have talked Buster into making a jump because this would not be something he would normally try. Because of that, no boxes were set up, and nobody volunteered to lie down. So he rode down the street past a couple of houses, turned into a driveway onto the sidewalk, and headed back our way, towards the ramp. His speed was slow at first, and then it was slow some more. After passing one house I believe the ramp got bigger in his eyes and fear began to grip him. Then he went from slow to slower, and as he hit the ramp we knew he was in trouble, but it was too late. We'd never seen anybody approach the ramp at such reduced speed so rather than call out for him to stop, I believe curiosity got the better of us and we all collectively refrained so we could see what would happen next. And so Buster Willis rolled slowly up that ramp with barely enough speed to make it to the top, eventually stopping when his bike frame got stuck at the apex, his front tire extended forward in midair and spinning slowly, his bike teetering, until he leaned forward, his front tire hitting the two-by-fours as he attempted to ride down the back side. But the downside was too steep, so he went over the handlebars, rolling to the ground below as his bike flipped on top of him.

There may have been snickers, but I don't remember laughter. First we had to make sure he was okay. He got up, and with all eyes on him, he dusted himself off, picked up his bike, and walked it home, and when he hit the garage he threw his bike down and started his familiar wail.

What made that event even more memorable was Mr. Ruhl's reaction. Apparently this level of spectacle compelled him to break all established parent/kid protocols by leaving his driveway to cross the street. He walked up to the ramp, looked it over, shook out his rag, and then looked down the street to Buster Willis's house. With a big smile on his face he said, "That's about the stupidest thing I've ever seen." It may have been the first time in the history of our neighborhood that our thinking aligned with an adult's.

Chris Garcia

Walk Like a Man

I started going to work with my dad when I was about eighteen months old. Around that time my mom bought me a plastic, red and yellow lawnmower to play with, and it quickly became my favorite toy. I must have thought that it really worked because my mom and older sisters told me that when my dad would mow the backyard, they would look out the window to see me walking right behind him in my saggy diaper, pushing my lawnmower just like him. My enthusiasm for mowing never waned, so by the time I was strong enough to push his mower my dad, recognizing an opportunity for solid, cheap labor, taught me how to mow the yard. He taught me to walk the yard first to pick up tree limbs or anything that might get caught in the blade and dull it, or worse, that might shoot out from the blade and injure me or someone else. He showed me how to put gas in the engine and how to check the oil, and he did it on concrete telling me that spilling either on the grass would kill it. Then he showed me how to set the levers and pull the rip cord, making sure that my feet were always clear of the machine. Lawnmowers were far more dangerous back then and people were losing fingers and toes when they mowed, so safety was always emphasized.

The handle to the mower had a bar halfway down that ran across the middle, and because I wasn't tall enough to get leverage on the top handle, I'd put one hand on it to steer and used the middle bar to push. If there was such thing as a self-propelled lawnmower at the time, nobody was using them. That's how I learned to mow, and I loved doing it, but I was around eight years old so I could only do it like that for the first few years, on the weekends, when Dad was home to supervise.

During the week, when he wasn't on the road or making sales calls, Dad would work in the warehouses and stockrooms of the companies that carried his Moog chassis parts. Sometimes, during the summer, Dad would take me or Dave to work with him, usually for an annual inventory count at a warehouse. Outings like this were always exciting for me because they were like doors to strange new adult worlds opening up for me, as if I were walking out of my world and into another dimension.

When we arrived, there was normally a lot of activity because other parts reps would be there to do their inventories as well. Dad would get there early and usually showed up with a box of donuts for the frontline people who worked the counters, where customers came in to order or buy their parts. They usually greeted him with a "Hey Joe!" or, "The Moog Man is here!" which shed a completely different light on him than I'd seen before. As we entered the warehouse I could tell that everybody knew everybody else because the other reps would greet him as well. He'd grab a cup of coffee and go around to say good morning to everybody and introduce me to them. After the introductions we'd go to the area of the warehouse where his parts were shelved and if any of the guys I'd met might have seemed different, he'd tell me why. If a guy had a scar on his face or was missing a finger, something a kid is going to notice, he'd tell me how it happened, maybe to satisfy my curiosity, or maybe so I wouldn't ask a stupid question out loud. One time I watched a man, who was obviously younger than the others, stroll in later than everyone else, with disheveled hair and wearing a full-length brown leather coat. He seemed to be well liked because some of the other men walked up to greet him and formed a small huddle as they joked around with him for a while. My dad saw that I was looking at him and told me that the guy in the leather jacket was popular with the ladies and that he liked to stay out late at night. That was all he said, but it did occur to me that we'd already been working for some time before he showed up.

The warehouses and stockrooms were usually poorly lit with concrete floors that were dirty and lined with 8' x 8' grey metal shelving that included six to eight shelves per section, depending on the size of the boxes they held. The aisles were just wide enough for two men to stand side by side, and to me they were like dark canyons where a kid could accidentally roam off and easily get lost. None of those places were air-conditioned, so the work was always hot and sweaty. I held the list and checked off the part numbers while Dad stood on his ladder calling them out, "K-242," and I'd say, "Check" and he'd say, "K-243" and I'd say, "Check" and we did that for hours. At night I'd go to bed and would still be counting those numbers in my dreams. Occasionally we'd stop and take a break and he'd take me to the red soda machine, the kind where the bottles were stacked in a single row and you opened the skinny little door to pull the ice-cold Coke or Dr. Pepper out of its slot, holding it in your hand with a desert in your mouth as droplets of condensation dripped down the sides of the light green glass. As if afraid that I was looking at a mirage I'd slowly lower the bottle to the little slot in the machine where the opener was to pop the metal top off and listen for that sound, pffft, catching just a subtle whiff of its exhaust. Those sodas lasted less than a minute but they were by far the greatest drinks I've ever had.

One time Dad took me out of town with him for an overnight "Changeover." A changeover was a pretty big deal for him because that meant he'd made a successful sale of his product to a warehouse distributor who was already carrying Moog's competitor's line of chassis parts. The trip meant that Dad would be substituting his parts for the incumbent's, who had now lost their place in the warehouse. That was always a big win for him. So we went to work and again he was on the ladder and I had the list. Sometimes we took turns, but again, this went on for hours. That night he took me to a local Italian restaurant, one with red checkered tablecloths on small, dark wooden tables. I was probably around twelve years old at the time and he let me order whatever I wanted. He ordered a medium pizza for himself, and I ordered a large pizza. He ate his and I ate mine. When we finished he asked me if I was still hungry and wanted anything else to eat and I said yes, so he let me order a medium pizza. A dark-haired woman, obviously the proprietor of the restaurant and one who was mother to all whom she met, came to our table with her notepad and had a good laugh about this skinny little kid ordering a second pizza, and by this time I think Dad was entertained to see if this was really going to happen. When the pizza was ready the nice lady brought it to our table and I made very short work of it, leaving no crust behind. We walked out of that place fat and happy. Later that night, as we lay side by side in our beds, wearing only our underwear, barely able to breathe, we looked over at each other to see hands rubbing and thumping rounded bellies that were tight as drums. That remained one of our fondest memories. We talked about going back years later to see if that restaurant was still there, but we never did.

Dad showed me how to change rubber washers that would stop leaky faucets. He showed me how to make repairs to my bicycle, and one time I helped him build a doghouse for Charlie Brown in our garage. Dad never lectured his boys about being responsible, about a work ethic, or about what it meant to be a man. He just showed us by walking his walk.

CARVEL DAZE

The Pinewood Derby

Dave and I spent enough time in the Cub Scouts to make it to the Webelos stage. One year Mom somehow found the time to be a Den Mother. The big annual event in Cub Scouts was the Pinewood Derby, a race between Scouts using cars fashioned from kits. True to its name, the kits included a block of pine wood, approximately six inches long, which would become the car body, four black plastic wheels, four nails to be used as axles, and number decals. The idea was for the Scouts to take one of those kits home and turn it into a race car.

The first year of participation, we entered Dave's car. I think he was in the Webelos at the time. We were completely new to this event and having no knowledge of what we were supposed to do, my dad, having the necessary skills to build such things, helped Dave construct his car. We went into the garage and Dad, like a wizard, pulled out his tools and showed us how to make a car out of a hunk of wood. He showed Dave how to shape the car and allowed him to use his power tools to grind the square edges and round them off to make it look similar to the car on the packaging. Then he showed Dave how to attach the axels, and because the car had to make a specific size and weight, he sent us out into the street to look for lead wheel weights, which he melted down in a pot over the stove. After that he showed Dave how to drill a hole into the bottom of the car, pour the lead into the opening, and then weigh and measure for accuracy. His instruction to Dave was precise in every detail and he inspected Dave's work for excellence. After that he left Dave to paint the car and add his favorite number. Dave finished it the night before the race.

Race day was held in a gymnasium and we were surprised to see that the place was buzzing with what seemed like over a hundred kids from dens and packs all over the city. The registration rules were very strict: First, the Scout had to be present to race his car, and upon arrival there was a set time for the car to be inspected and weighed. After that the car could not be altered. If your car did not pass inspection or was overweight, it was disqualified. The cars we saw were registered with all different sorts of shapes, colors, and designs, unlike the image on the box we had followed. Packs participated in tournament-style division events and the winners of those division events moved on to compete in an open division race for a winner-take-all race.

Long wooden tables were set up as ramps and two cars were placed on tracks side by side at the tops of the ramps and released. Some cars didn't even make it to the end of the track, but it didn't matter who won that heat. The cars were raced and timed again, this time switching tracks, and the best of the two times was recorded for each car. After each car in the division was raced and timed, a winner was declared.

I think Dave's car may have won in his pack's division, but it didn't win the overall, and for good reason. After we got a good look at the competition it was obvious that the other boys were getting a lot more influence with their dads' help than what ours had given, meaning, their dads were building the cars. Well, okey dokey, that's about all our pop needed to see.

The next year it was my turn. So, again, we went into the garage where the wizard pulled out his tools, and the three of us went back to work. This time Dad had some new ideas. This time, instead of a rounded front end, he had me ground the wood down until the hood sloped upwards, making it more aerodynamic. Then he instructed me to sand it down with three different grades of sandpaper, making it as smooth as possible. He sanded and polished the nail axels to make them perfectly smooth and had me apply graphite lubricant to them in order to reduce friction, which allowed the wheels to spin more freely. Then he left the car with me to paint. I painted mine blue and yellow, his company's colors. The year before, Dave's car came in a little underweight, and that made a difference, so this time Dad waited until the car was complete and the paint was dry and then, rather than getting in trouble again for ruining one of Mom's pots, he melted the lead weights down in a coffee can over the open fire of our stove top. After that we drilled a hole in the bottom of the car, slightly closer to the front this time, and then he carefully poured the lead in until the car hit the scale at exactly the maximum allowable weight. Everything he did was precise and according to the rules. The lead dried, I painted over it and then it was off to race day.

We took that car to the Pinewood Derby and smoked the competition. The races weren't even close. A few years after that, he and Landry repeated. Sorry, but you're just not going to beat a Moog Man and his sons with their Moog Cars on race day.

Chris Garcia

The Birth of Fire God

When we got bored, Dave and I would sometimes go into the garage to make "potions." Our potions consisted of anything we could find in a container sitting on a shelf, either liquid or solid, it didn't matter, as long as they could be mixed easily. Dave and I didn't collaborate often, but I believe he trusted me in our pursuit of alchemy because I had a natural inclination towards it, having proven myself by eating a chemistry set years earlier, and surviving. But luckily, we were not making our potions for consumption. We never actually made them for anything. We'd just find what we could, pour all the ingredients into a container, stir them up, and see what would happen. That was a potion. Sometimes I'd put a match to it afterwards to see if it would light. Usually it didn't. But one time it did.

Our dog, Charlie Brown, was a promising four hundred-meter sprinter whose track career got compressed and reduced to our backyard, which shortened his running distance significantly, but not his enthusiasm. After months of working out Charlie Brown had a dirt track cut into the grass along the fence line of our backyard where he would sometimes enjoy running sprints at full speed around and around the yard until it was time to start lifting weights. There was a large bush in the southeast corner of the yard, closest to the house, about the size of an igloo, with an entry way he used to go into to rest and escape from the sun. He went in and out of there so often that it eventually created a natural rounded doorway. His track either began or ended at that doorway, which was located on the north side of his bush. So that one fateful day, when Dave and I didn't have a place to dump our potion, we thought it would be a good idea to empty it at the edge of Charlie Brown's igloo. If his doorway was at twelve o'clock on that bush, then we poured our potion at 11:45, a quarter turn of the clock to the west of the hole, approximately ten feet from our house. But there was a problem. When we poured the potion out it left a big black spot, which would leave a stain or worse, kill the grass. Dad would see that when he mowed so we got the hose out and sprayed water on it, but that didn't help. So the kid who ate a chemistry set thought that it would be a good idea to perhaps burn the spot off. Out of curiosity, he lit it. And yeah, it worked. BIG TIME! In hindsight, we may have added a pinch of paint thinner or lighter fluid to that concoction, but it was too late, the flames shot up and the bush began to burn. We looked at each other in complete shock, and then we looked at the house. But we didn't panic. We had the hose out already, so we turned it on and with great confidence, sprayed the flame. To our great surprise the water created a larger, and more immediate problem because apparently we'd added oil to this particular potion, and even though they say oil and water don't mix, fire likes it when they try, so the fire became inspired, and grew dramatically. Luckily my dad had a pile of sand in our backyard at the time, so we heaped some of it on the fire, which finally extinguished the beast. But that left another problem for us: now there was a giant burn mark on the ground, and a very noticeable part of the west side of the bush had burnt off. It was late afternoon, which meant at least one of our parents would be home soon. The Informers hadn't seen anything yet, so we grabbed a shovel and some hedge trimmers, dug out the burned grass, and smoothed it over with sand, then we cut the burned limbs and leaves away, leaving a nice, rounded doorway for Charlie Brown. Now his bush had matching front *and* back doors!

Incredibly, nobody ever asked about the bush. And as it turned out, the new design was no problem for Charlie Brown—he adjusted to it quickly by incorporating the additional doorway into a new workout routine. With our heat-treated modification, he now had a tunnel in the backyard to run through.

But my career with fire had already been established by then. Years earlier, after my Kansas City-klepto phase and shortly after my chemical-eating phase, I took a turn at playing with matches. Nobody realized it then but apparently I was developing into an elemental guy whose emerging preferences ran on the hot side. So I snuck matches whenever I could, took them to a hiding place, and lit them. Then I would simply watch them burn before blowing them out. Well, one day I wanted to see what would happen if I put the flame to the cuff of a shirt hanging in one of the closets upstairs. Would it burn? I lit the match and set it under the cuff of a white dress shirt and . . . mystery solved! Answer: Yes, it will! What's more, and much to my wide-eyed dismay, the shirt took the flame quite readily and it became immediately, and shockingly, evident that perhaps starch was an unknown friend of fire, as its properties appeared to be an exceedingly effective accelerant towards its cause. This created a problem because the flame started to grow and I couldn't blow it out, and then it started to spread . . . quickly. Another shirt started to catch fire so I panicked and called for help. Luckily one of my older sisters was nearby and stepped in to put it out, leaving smoke throughout the upstairs and black scorch marks on the back of the closet and pole.

It was early in the day when that happened, and I knew I was in huge trouble—that life was, in fact, over for me. My sister looked at me like the sentence had been handed down and the hangman was already riding into town. I was a dead man walking. There was nothing left for me to do now but run away. So I went to my room to pack but I wasn't old enough to have my own suitcase, so I went hobo. I removed the cover from my pillow and started stuffing essentials into it: my baseball glove, fake dog-doo, the two-week-old jawbreaker that I was still working on, my yo-yo, and other indispensable sundries like that. When it was full another one of my older sisters came in with a small suitcase and gave it to me. It was a solemn exchange, I knew, because as she put the suitcase on my bed she looked at me, said nothing, and walked away. I could tell she would miss me. I filled that suitcase with clothes and went downstairs for some food. By now the word had spread, and they were all waiting for me there, looking at me for the last time as I entered the dining room with that dark cloud of imminent doom hanging over my head. My grandmother even had two bologna sandwiches ready-made. She handed me the brown paper bag, slowly, with a sadness in her eyes, and said goodbye. I knew she would miss me too. So I thanked her and put the bag in my pillow case. It was time to go. Crying, I said goodbye to her and to all of my brothers and sisters, and walked out the front door and down the block, to where? Without a raft or a nearby river, I did not know.

Later in life, as an adult, my friends called me Pyro Man or Fire God, or FG for short, because I could build campfires that were visible from the International Space Station.

The Institution

The first day of school was always the worst day of the year. It meant the end of summer and the beginning of a nine-month prison sentence. And going out to buy school supplies? That was like going to the grocery store to buy liver for dinner. I still get sick to my stomach when I see back to school ads.

Entering our elementary school was like walking into the warm embrace of a bomb shelter. Everything about the structure was institutional, from the cold, grey walls made of cinder block, to the cold, grey speckled floor tile, to the cold, grey wardens running The Institution. The walls were decorated with numbers, and with letters of the alphabet, in large block print, and with lists of rules. That was it. Our school principal was R. B. DeVille, or as we called him, Rubber Butt DeVille. Not sophisticated as a nickname, but that's about as clever as elementary-aged kids get with a burn. He was a nervous, gruff, and mean-spirited man; short, wiry, and dark-haired with a small black mustache, and he always wore a dark suit, white shirt, and a black tie. He instilled fear throughout the school by calling out any indiscretion, or perceived indiscretion, or by spontaneously quizzing kids using the most dastardly methods.

It was bad news when RB walked into a classroom. Before he entered, the only sound in the room may have been pencils writing on notebook paper, but when he came in even the mice gasped, and then everything got deadly silent. He'd stroll in, look the room over, write something on the chalkboard, and pace up and down the aisles without saying a word until all of a sudden he'd whip around and heave the eraser at the chalkboard where it would hit in an explosion of white dust. Other times he'd stare the children down until he selected his victim and would stop at their desk, ordering the trembling innocent to stand up and recite their times tables. May God have mercy on your poor soul if you were ever sent into the hall to stand and face the wall for disrupting class. Abject fear and trepidation would overtake you as you looked left and right, hoping the crypt keeper would turn the corner and walk down the hall to end things before Mr. DeVille had his chance. One time he stopped my sister Sharon out on the playground and pop-quizzed her on our mom's maiden name. An elementary school kid knows their mother's maiden name the same way they know their periodic table. His favorite, though, was personally threatening students with detention. He did it suddenly, and you never knew if you were going to be next. "That's five days after school! Not one, not two, not three, not four, but five! Five days after school!" He'd put a fist up in front of a kid's face and lift a finger with every day he counted down. One time I saw him lean over a redheaded kid and perform the countdown because the little ingrate dropped a book and stepped out of line to pick it up. What a charmer.

In the mornings we used to gather in front of the school and wait for the bell to ring at 8:00 before entering. Some mornings, on a whim, or if it was cold or raining outside, Rubber Butt would assemble the students in the auditorium before the bell rang. The auditorium had a stage, but it also served as the school lunchroom. The tables were set up just before lunchtime and the floor would be empty when we'd enter, so we would all file in and stand, facing the stage. He would take the stage on those mornings, grab the microphone, and begin to sing two of his old favorites to the entire student body. Imagine Hitler singing "Streets of Laredo." It was inspiring. He was, for the record, the only person who could turn "Buffalo Gals" into an angry song. His voice was like gravel in a cement mixer, and he had all the stage presence of a disjointed marionette, but to his credit, the little despot could carry a tune.

In church I once heard the preacher talking about knowing a tree by its fruit. As a kid I didn't know if nuts grew on trees, or whether they were considered fruit. But I didn't need to be a Bible expert to get the drop on that guy. Some things you just know.

Our teachers, the wardens of The Institution, seemed to follow RB's lead. This was a lineup of hard women who no doubt looked forward to scaring children on Halloween night. This wasn't Catholic school so they couldn't carry rulers to rap your knuckles, but their severe countenance and witchy ways served them just as well. These wardens didn't smile, and they weren't interested in making learning fun. Their job was to grab a power tool and drill knowledge into your head from 8:00 a.m. until 3:00 p.m. every single day. Gosh that was fun. I was not at all interested in what they had to say so I learned how to multiply by counting the vertical tiles on the ceiling and multiplying by the number of horizontal tiles. I entertained myself in other ways, but I pretty much spent the rest of my time looking out the window and waiting for the bell to ring. I never raised my hand, and if I was ever called on for an answer, I never knew it. Sometimes that would be embarrassing. After all, you never want to get caught with your participles dangling in front of the entire classroom. But if the warden had ever said something like, "Mickey Mantle went to bat a hundred times and got thirty-five hits. What percentage of time did he get a hit?" Well, I *could* have been a mathematical genius!

It seems like all of my brothers and sisters excelled in school, especially my sisters. But my sisters always seemed to look forward to that first day. I guess because they would get reacquainted with friends that they may not have seen all summer. It also meant that they got to wear their new clothes. At that time, my parents hadn't hit their stride financially so we got new clothes at the beginning of the school year, and that was it, except for maybe Christmas. Clothes didn't mean anything to me, probably because I sometimes had to wear hand-me-downs, and because I was really hard on anything new, so my mom would buy me Toughskin jeans. This particular line of denims made their own unique fashion statement. The fabric was thick and permanently starched, and the legs were reinforced by large stiff patches that covered the entire knee area from three inches above the knees to three inches below. It was like walking in sandpaper. It sounded like it, too. The statement was: you're a dork. But those jeans lived up to their name. They were tough alright, and they lasted. But they were hard to break in. Usually I wasn't able to bend my legs completely until mid-October.

One of the worst days of the school year was report card day. Back then, The Institution sent kids home with their report cards to get a parent's signature and return them back to the classroom warden. The report card was a simple half piece of thick white paper, like construction paper, that folded open like a book. On the left side the subjects were listed and graded A-F, and on the right side were more behavioral descriptions like **Pays Attention** or **Gets Along Well With Others**. Those were graded with (+) or (-) signs. In our house, As were expected and Bs were only tolerated under extreme circumstances, like a sudden bout of death. On the right side of the ledger, (-) signs might be answered by Mom's paddle. My report cards were typically defiled with Cs, Ds, and the occasional B. The miracle A rarely graced the left side of that ledger. But by around the third or fourth grade, after being swatted and grounded twice a year for the first several years of my scholastic career, I came home with another travesty of the educational system, handed my mom The Institution's warrant for my death sentence, whereupon she opened it, smiled, and said, "Well, son, if you can't dazzle 'em with your brilliance, baffle 'em with your BS." I guess she thought I'd earned a college degree already because she never punished me for another report card after that.

I knew my mom was kidding me in a warm kind of way as she signed the card and maybe surrendered to the scholastic reality of her #5. I think Mom knew that I hated school and recognized my academic limitations. She knew that I was a dreamer and a romantic at heart. A little later in life she called me her Don Quixote son. I figured that one out later, but I think she had a pretty good read on me early on.

In the middle of my fifth-grade year we got a new teacher. I think one of the wardens was transferred to Russia to run a gulag, a demotion in my estimation. But her replacement was a man. And not just any kind of man. Her replacement was a black man named Mr. Wiltz, the coolest teacher of all time. We called him Wiltz the Stiltz. This nickname was just plain lazy since Wilt Chamberlain already owned that name. But this guy looked like the young version of Sidney Poitier, only he was more athletic, and maybe a little taller. And the best thing was, he was nice! He was always well dressed, very sharp in his white, long-sleeved button-down shirt with cuffs rolled up once, tie, slacks, and pretty stylish looking loafers. These were not my dad's shoes. It was not unusual to see Mr. Wiltz talking with his students in the hall or showing them a few basketball moves during recess. He was a gentle man, and he was a gentleman. And shockingly, he smiled, a lot. He was fun! Everybody wanted him as a teacher. And I got him the next year, when I entered the sixth grade.

Okay, so this story is not going to turn into *To Sir, with Love*. Mr. Wiltz did not change my life or turn me into a good student, so a movie deal about his time at The Institution is not forthcoming here. I mention him because he made an impression on me. He was a good English teacher. He obviously enjoyed teaching, he cared about his students, and he managed to elevate my English skills from mediocre to less mediocre. I left that school the next year and I heard that he left two years after that. Too bad, because he was the best thing that ever happened to The Institution.

It was at that school, in the sixth grade, that a guy whom I considered one of my best friends—Roger—called me a spick. At that time we didn't have any Hispanic kids in our class, at least none that I recall, and I never identified myself as being Hispanic.

My parents certainly didn't teach us to think that way. Our last name was something to be proud of, to be worn like a flag or family badge, so as for me, we were all the same. I'd heard the word spick used before, but it never occurred to me that the Garcia name might be considered different. So what he said was a shock to me. I knew what that name meant, and I didn't like hearing it because it made me feel like I was somehow different and lower than him. We were in the bathroom and there was another kid in there with us, but there wasn't any fighting or teasing going on. His name-calling seemingly came out of nowhere, so when he said it, I was stunned and didn't even look at him. I was confused and wondered where that came from. It was the first and only time anyone ever called me by that name.

Besides recess the only good thing about school were the spontaneous pauses in our studies. Fire drills were always fun because they were designed to get us outside quickly. That worked for me because *I* was designed to get outside quickly. A couple times we had bomb threats called in, so those were better because they lasted longer, some for more than an hour. Nothing ever happened, of course. Just some kid calling in a prank, no doubt. And no, surprisingly, it wasn't me. And then of course, there were the nuclear bomb drills where we had to duck and cover under our desks for protection or line up along the walls of the halls and do the same. If those desks couldn't protect us from Rubber Butt, how were they supposed to protect us from a bomb?

The Institution was so bad that my parents pulled Landry from that dark asylum in the fifth grade and sent him to a magnet school. I always admired him for getting out. It was the greatest escape!

Chris Garcia

Tricks & Treats, Night & Day

My oldest sister, Vicki, holds two master's degrees. An enthusiast in education and someone who actually enjoyed going to school, she was passionate about literature and learning and encouraged us to start reading at an early age. She usually exerted this influence during the absolute worst time by waking us up early on some random summer morning and marching us down to the library. This made no sense to me. School was out. Summer was in, and the world was right. What was she thinking? Why was I even awake?

For the uninitiated, a library is a building with many books that you can borrow and take home. It's weird. I guess she took us there so our brains wouldn't get dry and rusty over the summer. Whatever her motivation was, I learned early on that she and I weren't just from different planets, we orbited different stars. On these occasional summer mornings, Vicki would line us younger ones up to make the two-mile trip by foot to Walter Branch Library. So she'd get us out of bed, making sure we got properly dressed and put together, and off to The Wizard we'd go, under the late morning sun, walking in a line down the sidewalk like baby ducks following their mother. It was half a block as a crow flies to get out of our neighborhood so after walking down past

Bob's house to the end of our block it was a left and two quick rights and then it was a straight shot up a busy street, under the freeway, and past a few brand-new fast food restaurants so that by the time we got to the library we were pretty much humidity-steamed and sunbaked, medium rare. I was never impressed with being woken to make that Bataan Death March, but once we got to the library I was free to wander around and pick out any books that I wanted, so that lifted my spirits a little. It didn't take long for me to find the sports section where I'd roam and settle on a book about Mickey Mantle or the "say hey kid," Willie Mays. I didn't want to be greedy, so I'd only check out one at a time. Besides, one thin book was also a good fit for the walk home.

Vicki had a job by this time, which meant she had *money*, so sometimes she'd line us up after dinner and escort us for the half-mile duck walk to Baskin-Robbins for ice cream, her treat. Now here was a hike I could get behind and support! I believe we moseyed on over in the shade rather easily for those trips, or maybe we sauntered, we may have even skipped a little, but whatever we did, that walk was *more like it*!

There were some things we were doing for fun as kids that eventually turned into popular professional sports. Skateboards, for instance, only began being manufactured in the mid-1960s, and their use didn't catch on until the mid-70s. Motocross didn't start to become popular in the US until roughly the same time. While we didn't have motorcycles, we did clip baseball cards to our spokes to make it sound like we did. But we were doing tricks on skateboards and our bikes on a regular basis starting in the late 60s.

Before skateboarding became popular, we had silver metal skates with silver metal wheels, the kind that you slipped your shoe into and wore like stainless steel sandals, with a fitted heel and leather strap that wrapped around your ankle and two metal pincers that clamped your pinky and big toes down. With a key you could turn a corkscrew shaft that tightened the pincers and squeezed all your toes together like a vice grip. That must be what it feels like to walk in high heels. Hard to imagine improving on such a well-thought-out instrument of kid torture, so we stripped down the evil design and came up with our own innovation. We'd remove the metal wheels from our skates, find a hunk of wood in the garage, cut it into a skateboard shape, glue some sandpaper to the top for traction, and attach the metal wheels to the other side. Unfortunately, those boards didn't corner well as the wheels only scraped the cement when you went into a turn, and because the metal wheels offered no traction the ride was loose and slippery so attempting any type of trick, like a one-eighty, was an invitation to a concrete faceplant, and pretty much an act of suicide. So the best thing to do would be to grab a rope and have someone drag you down the street on it behind their bike.

Clay wheels made a short appearance, but they were still too hard to grip the cement so maneuvering on them offered little improved traction. It felt more like riding on gravel. Skateboards with urethane wheels would follow several years later and Bill Layton would end up being the true master surfer of the skateboard. By the mid-70s he was already riding the pipes along a nearby concrete bayou or carving up empty swimming pools he'd find in the neighborhood. He was doing that at least as early as anybody in California.

I'm told that when my dad started dating my mother that they'd take walks around her block during his visits, and that he'd sometimes walk around the block on his hands while they talked. I guess genes matter because standing on my hands to see how far I could walk was something I liked to do, probably because I heard that story. I do know that I didn't stick with it long enough to make it all the way across our front yard, not because I lost interest, but because I figured out a way to ride my skateboard on my hands. So I'd hold my board on both ends as I ran sideways, rolling the board on the ground for maybe ten feet until I had enough speed to throw my legs up and ride. I could get as far as down the driveway and across our sidewalk to the next driveway and into the street before running out of momentum.

I also used to enjoy jumping ramps on my bike or riding wheelies down the street. The furthest I ever rode a wheelie was halfway down my block. But there was nothing spectacular about doing stuff like that in our neighborhood. Everybody could ride and we all had skills. And because we were outside all day playing a myriad of sports and games, we were athletic, we were well coordinated, and we had great balance—we were adept and competent kids. Safety helmets weren't even a twinkle in anybody's eyes because they weren't necessary. Their popular use didn't emerge for decades. Not a single kid on our block busted his head open doing the things we did. Yeah, we scraped a few elbows and knees, but just like a broken chain or a blown out inner tube on our bikes, we knew how to patch those up on our own.

And those baseball cards? Nobody collected them for any kind of financial gain, and nobody was taking them to autograph shows, because there was no such thing. There was no autograph market. Most of the cards in a pack were the same crummy players that always cycled through, but occasionally we'd score a Bob Gibson or Roberto Clemente, so we collected and traded those baseball cards for the prestige. They cost less than a dime a dozen and were packaged with a thin piece of pink chewing gum that was so stiff and stale that it snapped and crumbled like a communion wafer, or like a sliver of hard plastic left out in the sun for too long. It was so dry that it took a full minute to soften enough to chew after putting it in your mouth. But there's no telling what those spoked cards would be worth today. We'll never know because one day Dave and I went to our closets to get our shoebox collections and they were gone. We couldn't say for sure but we suspected Mom chunked them during one of her more radical spring cleanings.

Snowboarding is an Olympic sport and would not exist today without the early popularity of the skateboard. And motocross would not have gained in popularity if kids weren't making daredevil jumps on their bicycles first. So if Evel Knievel might be considered the morning star of what would eventually become the X Games, an extreme competition for the truly fearless, then just maybe we were part of its emergent dawning light. But we were fearless, too, and maybe even a little bit crazy.

We had this very unusual game we played called Join in the Spirit of Fun. Nobody knows where it originated and no one ever stepped forward to make the claim of inventing it, but it was just another example of us kids creating spontaneous stupidity. For this game everyone was involved, both boys and girls, from Dave's age on down and it could take place anywhere—in a bedroom, a yard, the garage, it didn't matter. It was a rarity for all of us to be playing together so it took a game like tag or hide-and-seek to get us assembled. You never knew when or if it was going to happen but if the game we were playing started to slow down or get boring, someone would suddenly call out, "join in the spirit of fun!" This was the cue for us to initiate our own version of mayhem, so we would all freeze in place, look at each other in wide-eyed shock, and then we would break out into a free-for-all fake rumble. Things would get crazy very easily after that. In less than a minute we would have mattresses and pillows pulled out of our bedrooms and dragged into the front yard. A pillow fight would break out; somebody would launch someone else in the air by swinging a Hippity Hop at them; fake barroom brawls ensued where guys flipped guys over their shoulders, landing them on the ground; one fighter would toss another out of a tree to land on the mattresses. Meanwhile a neighbor's car would slowly roll by, a confused look on the occupant's faces as they tried to make sense of this picture show of deranged lunatics. Did I ever mention anything about *Lord of the Flies*?

On some occasions, in the summertime only, we were allowed to play outside at night. I suspect this was allowable only after Mom's and Dad's nerves were so completely shot that they just wanted us out of the house, but the Big Girls were usually out in the neighborhood talking with their friends at night, so that probably had something to do with it as well. Sometimes we played hide-and-seek, but playing that game at night was much different than playing it during the day. At night we took the game much more seriously.

One time I decided I was going to elevate my stealth game, so I went into my room and dressed myself in the darkest clothes I had, then I went into my dad's dresser and pulled out a pair of his black dress socks and slipped them over my white tennis shoes. Then I got out his shoe polish and painted my face black. After that I slipped on a black stocking cap and went outside.

It "wasn't fair" to hide around the corner of our street or in a backyard at night so we had to set boundaries for this game, limiting them to a specific area that would span a half block of front yards and houses, but all options were open after that. You could hide in bushes, in trees, under cars, on tops of houses, and since many garage doors were often still open at night, anywhere in there was fair game as well. Our street was dark at night with streetlights so dimly lit and spread out that you could lie on the cool grass in the summertime and gaze out at a billion twinkling diamonds, high up in the sky. So the stage was set.

A tree, centrally located in someone's front yard, would be home base. If you were the seeker, you had to stand at that tree and count to fifty with your hands over your eyes, then you could start seeking. The littler ones hadn't figured out that sound travelled yet, and they usually didn't stray too far from that tree so if you heard them rustle or snicker you would leave them alone to keep the game moving. Sometimes the older girls would help the younger kids find a good hiding spot, and eventually they'd get better at finding their own. But as soon as the seeker wandered off they'd typically pop out of their spot and race to home base, victorious! If a younger kid did get tagged, they'd usually group up with others their age to look for the older ones, or one of the older ones would help them seek. But that didn't happen very often.

We were all very skilled seekers because we knew every nook and cranny of our neighborhood, but conditions changed at night so finding a hider could take five minutes or more because we also knew how to be creative about finding new places to hide. If you did find someone, you had to touch them before they could get to home base and if you did that successfully, you would call out, "you're it!" as you touched them so everyone could hear. After that the new "it" person would have to go to the tree to count to fifty while you ran away to find a place to hide.

We were quiet as Indians playing that game and never got chased away by a neighbor, so they either never heard us while we were on their property, or they heard us and didn't care. We'd be out there playing sometimes until past 10:00 and then, suddenly, there came the whistle. All of our evening or night games ended with a father's whistle. That was the signal to come home, and each dad had his own signature sound. The first whistle usually came from Mr. Tucker, Jay's dad. His was a three-note trill lasting several seconds that sounded more like something from a songbird. His was by far the best and most melodic. Mr. Ruhl's and Mr. Layton's whistles were also unique, employing one or two rising and falling notes. Dad's was the shortest because he had little time for symphonies. His was a single-note burst, more like, "fweet!" All of the whistles traveled to the end of our block and it didn't matter what you were doing when the call home sounded; you stopped or dropped whatever you were doing and ran home. That was the drill and it was non-negotiable.

But being out late at night was not a big deal in terms of safety though, so it was not unusual for us to be out when it was dark. At the time it was normal for me to walk or ride my bike home from a night game at Bayland if I didn't have a ride. It was also normal to kick a single rock all the way home without any thought of a bad guy. That isn't to say that there was no such thing as bad apples, though.

Ghouls and goblins ruled Halloween night and you just didn't know what one of them might do. On rainy days in summer when we couldn't play baseball or go to the pool we'd play Nerf baseball indoors at Bob's house, if his mom was working that day, but mostly we'd play ping-pong in his garage. And it was in the garage, around August, that our Halloween preparations began.

They called it trick or treat for a reason, and we took the trick part very seriously. In late summer we'd start slowly by incrementally gathering newspapers, toilet paper, and soap and hiding them in our secret places. If we were playing ping-pong then at least four of us, Bob, me, Bill and Dave, would be in the garage, two of us volleying while the other two cut up newspapers into tiny squares and dropped them into lawn bags. Bob's garage was a small "one car" so after filling a bag we'd have to take it to our house and find a place to hide it. One or two bags would be enough for our trick.

One time I had a dental appointment in the early evening leading into Halloween night, which to me was like taking a bath before going out to play in the mud. As I looked out the car window on the ride home I could see that the sun was starting to go down, which made me very anxious, this being the second greatest night of a kid's life, next to Christmas Eve, so I was getting a little sick to my stomach. Is that "The Monster Mash" playing on the radio? Why am I still stuck in this car on my way home from the dentist? Why isn't this car moving? Step on it, lady!

At six or seven years old, kids loved to get their store-bought Halloween costumes. I remember one year Bob was dressed in full costume as Shazaan, complete with a blinking light on his head. Our family used to get costumes at the five-and-dime, mask only. We had to improvise to complete the effect. I didn't get a mask that dreadful year of the dentist visit so for that night I put on some of my dad's old clothes, scratched charcoal onto my face, and applied some fake blood on my head and around my mouth to look like a bum who just got rolled. Some kids just don't think things through. I guess I was going more for emotional complexity than fear in the development of my character.

During that time, rumors and warnings swirled about sick-minded people putting razor blades in apples. Whether that was myth or not made no difference—it was no threat to us. Who eats an apple on Halloween night? What kid even allows one to occupy that kind of space in their bag? If it was coated with candy or caramel, it would be saved for later. If it was just an apple or some other piece of fruit, we'd treat it like it was an affront to our sensibilities, chunk it down the block, and watch until it exploded in the street. Hey, the birds have to eat too.

The first order of business on Halloween night was to secure the candy, so we'd go door to door, up one street and down another for several blocks until our bags were full. Some people would set up their homes as haunted houses so we'd walk through the dark, black curtain-lined hallways, putting our hands through an opening to feel our way into a bowl of cold wet brains. The spooky sounds of chains being dragged and people screaming in fear would be playing as we crept down the corridor, just waiting for someone to jump out at us from around the next dark corner. It was not cool to react in fear, but with each step forward we always knew our doom was imminent.

After that we'd go home and inventory our loot: a speckle-colored jawbreaker, like a round robin's egg, about the size of a ping-pong ball that you'd put in your mouth to work on, tucking it into your cheek during the day and putting it on your bed post at night, right after your head hit the pillow, to save for the next day; a SweeTart brick, the size of a hockey puck, that you had to gnaw on like a rat all day to finish; and all of the various chocolate bars that we broke into and finished off greedily. Suddenly the trip to the dentist made more sense.

Then it was time. Time to put our summer preparations to work. So, we'd stuff our pockets with the bars of soap and gather our bags of cut up newspaper and rolls of toilet paper and proceed to decorate the neighborhood by spreading our confetti on the lawns, soaping house and car windows, and wrapping trees with toilet paper. If it was humid or it rained overnight, cleanup would be a problem for the victim the next day. On the upside, perhaps newspaper clippings doubled as a quality mulch. Who knew? You just had to keep a positive attitude and look on the bright side.

When Halloween ended, the calendar turned and November arrived, which meant Thanksgiving was up ahead, which really meant Santa was on the horizon.

Chris Garcia

Christmastime

The holidays were such a special time for our family, mainly because of Mom, who lived for that time of year as much as her kids did. Dad received his year-end bonus right around Christmas, and because the two of them had to be so penny-wise all the time, this was the one time of the year when they could splurge a little. And when I say they had to count their pennies, I mean, for instance, lots of oatmeal for breakfast instead of cereals. If we did get cereal, it usually wasn't your Cap'n Crunch or Froot Loops but the generic brands with no logos or designs on the packaging, just names like Puffs, which came in large plastic bags with no box to contain it. Sometimes we had to use powdered milk, which was dehydrated white milk powder in a box that you mixed with tap water to create a thin, grey tasteless liquid with lumps that you either drank, or poured over your generic cereal. As an alternative we would sometimes break up pieces of bread in a bowl, pour milk over it, and sprinkle with sugar and cinnamon. It was, in the vernacular of the day, a drag, man. Maybe we didn't always have everything we wanted throughout the year, but we did have everything we needed. Powdered milk was a drag, but it's all we had sometimes. I think it was a drag for my mom to bring home as well, so she always made Christmastime a feel-good time for all of us.

For our family the holidays started on Thanksgiving Day when we woke to the sounds of the Macy's Thanksgiving Day Parade in full regalia on the living room TV; to the music of one of Mom's favorite Christmas albums playing softly in the background; to the smells of pumpkin pies already baked and sitting out to cool; and to the thirty-two-pound turkey roasting in the oven. That's when the anticipation of Santa began.

The birds Mom brought home from the grocery store every year were so big that they barely fit in the oven, and it's not an exaggeration to say that she had to set hers out for two days just to thaw. Then she would yank out all the guts, rinse it, season it, and stuff it. And to make sure the turkey was cooked all the way through by dinnertime, she'd set the oven at 350 degrees and put the turkey in right after Halloween.

Entering the living room to the holiday sounds and smells she created only happened once a year and always signaled to me that a change was in the air. On that day, walking through the doorways of our bedrooms was like transitioning through a fairy dust-sprinkled portal that left behind the humdrum of our everyday lives, releasing us into the beginnings of the mystical magic and wonder of the Christmas season that had yet to unfold.

Mom was always excited about the Macy's Thanksgiving Day Parade, it was a big annual event nationwide, so we all gathered around the TV to watch the great college marching bands, the themed floats with dancers and singers waving, the giant Underdog, Snoopy, and Mickey Mouse balloons that filled the entire street corridor as they drifted along and edged the skyscrapers that bordered it, and ultimately the big finale, Santa's first appearance of the year. But our stomachs were confused. They weren't used to smelling dinner and dessert in the morning. It made us hungry, but the kitchen was OCCUPIED, so we had to adopt new methods to get breakfast. It was guerrilla warfare on Thanksgiving morning, and we always risked injury just to get something to eat. We had to dart in to grab dry cereal or a tortilla and dart out without being scolded for being in the way or we would risk taking a hit to the back of the leg with the flyswatter. Stopping to pour a glass of milk, powdered or otherwise, was unthinkable. There simply wasn't enough time for a *leche* fix. When the parade was over, college football would come on TV, so I'd go outside and meet up with Bob and the neighborhood kids for a game until later in the afternoon, when I'd go in to watch the next game with Dad.

Dad's job for Thanksgiving was to watch football, drink a rare beer or two, and carve the turkey at dinnertime. It was the only time of year I ever saw him sit down and relax. I remember one time his boss, Mr. Reamer, was in town and dropped by for a Thanksgiving day visit. It was early afternoon and shortly after he arrived, for some reason, Mr. Reamer fainted and crumpled to the floor right in our living room, probably after seeing the size of our family and trying to process the activity buzzing all around him. He was okay and left shortly thereafter, apologizing for cutting his visit short and looking a little embarrassed. I guess some people just panic when they find themselves inside of a tornado.

Whether we had guests or not, the Christmas season was the time of year when I had to be on my absolute best behavior. I realized that I could get a little naughty during the months leading up to the holidays and as a consequence, by November, I usually had a jacket full of unsubstantiated charges and alleged indiscretions that usually had me stacking time in solitary (grounded to my room). But after Thanksgiving I knew I had to clean up my act because I knew The Big Man was watching (this was before Clarence Clemons), so I was on my best behavior to remain in good standing regarding The List.

Sometimes when I was home and under one of my older sisters' care I would accidentally misbehave or somehow get on their nerves. I don't know if they were allowed to spank me or not, but they couldn't send me to my room and make me stay, so if my offense was particularly egregious, they'd pull out their big gun and call Santa. The effectiveness of this behavioral modification technique was directly proportional to the month of the year: the closer to Christmas, the more effective it would be. I didn't pay much mind to their threats if they made them in the summer but by around mid-November they had my attention, and by the time the calendar flipped to December and Christmas grew near, I became fearful because by then my letter had been mailed and I knew that the fat man was making his list and checking it twice, in earnest.

The threat usually involved one of the persecutors making the call from the downstairs phone with maybe a boyfriend on the upstairs phone playing the part of Santa. I wasn't aware of the scheme at the time but at this point they had my full attention. Santa was one of four people that I dared not lie to (the others being my parents and Jesus). Somehow the four of them could always tell, so with family members staring at me and the phone shaking in my hand, Santa read off the charges against me, and with trembling, apocalyptic visions of a stocking filled with hard black coal I confessed readily, apologized, and sent myself to my room. After an hour or two I'd come back out, and that usually settled it, until the next time. But I never felt like I was on solid footing as Christmas neared so by mid-December I was volunteering for chores and pulling out chairs for my sisters at the dinner table. I was the kid who usually had to rely on bonus points and extra credit to get by, so I took no chances.

We usually went shopping for our Christmas tree right after Thanksgiving, and because this was not a decision for amateurs, Mom always picked it out. She preferred the Scotch pine or the Douglas fir—the bigger the better. Of course, she had to haggle with Dad to get the eight-foot tree that would fan out to four or five feet in diameter, but she always won those negotiations. Mom also did all of the Christmas present shopping and didn't run anything by Dad in the process, so she would always hear it from him when the bills came due afterwards. But Mom was a kid during the holidays, so she didn't ever pay much attention to his pecuniary particulars that time of year. They had the same conversation every year, and I could never figure out why he even attempted to parley with her because he never won, and he never won because she was not going to negotiate at Christmastime. She was clever because she knew that she had to pick her battles when it came to money during the year, but during the holidays if she wanted something, she was going to get it, even if it meant walking right through his objections.

One year we departed from our traditional tree and tried out a blue spruce, but after being in the house for about two weeks it suddenly gave up the ghost and entered into a surprising death spiral. The tree was directly to the left as you entered the front door, and the first sign of trouble was when the draft created by the door opening and closing made the dying pine needles cascade down the tree, giving the wrapped presents below a dry, crispy sprinkle that was audible from several feet away. A week later that sprinkle turned into brown rain, which was *no bueno* for Mom, so we carefully removed the decorations, chunked the tree in the backyard, and had a new one up and decorated that evening.

Between Thanksgiving and Christmas Day the pile of wrapped presents under the tree grew incrementally larger and larger until they spilled out into a stack that eventually grew three feet high, completely surrounding the tree, like a castle wall. The sight was always a shock to our friends when they came over because none of them had ever seen anything like it before. As soon as they entered the house, they would become paralyzed, stupefied— they'd never seen that many presents at one time—so I could see the wheels start turning as they began doing the math in their heads and thinking: how could Santa even fit that many presents in one bag? These were the mysteries we all had to contend with.

And then there were the cartoons that were absolute must-watch TV, especially the big five classics: *A Charlie Brown Christmas*, *Frosty the Snowman*, *How the Grinch Stole Christmas*, *Santa Claus Is Coming to Town*, and *Rudolph the Red-Nosed Reindeer*—the last two productions done in Claymation. These were huge annual television events, and all kids everywhere knew when they were scheduled to air so there was no way we would miss them. There was a progression towards Christmas Day, and for us watching those animated classics was part of the countdown. They were some of the essential steps along the way to the big day.

But it was always Mom's music that really set the atmosphere for the season. She had so many Christmas albums, including collections from Goodyear and Firestone that were sold in gas stations every year for a dollar (no purchase necessary) and contained the works of the greatest orchestras, choirs, and vocalists of her era including Mitch Miller, Nelson Eddy, André Previn, Percy Faith, the Mormon Tabernacle Choir, and Leonard Bernstein and the New York Philharmonic Orchestra. She collected those albums every year during the 60s and they were our family favorites. They included immense vocal talents who sang what would become household signature songs that were among the greatest of what would grow into enduring classics, such as:

Bing Crosby – "White Christmas" / "The White World of Winter"
Gene Autry – "Santa Claus Is Comin' to Town"
Barbra Streisand – "Silent Night"/ "Ave Maria"/ "The Lord's Prayer"
Andy Williams – "Do You Hear What I Hear"/" O Holy Night" / "It's the Most Wonderful Time of the Year"
Tony Bennett – "I've Got My Love to Keep Me Warm"
Steve Lawrence & Eydie Gorme – "Let It Snow" / "Sleigh Ride"
Mahalia Jackson – "Away in a Manger"
Johnny Mathis – "Christmas Is" / "A Marshmallow World"
Sammy Davis Jr. – "Jingle Bells" / "It's Christmas All Over the World"

Mario Lanza – "O Come, All Ye Faithful"
Doris Day – "Toyland" / "Silver Bells"
Robert Goulet and Carol Lawrence – "The Christmas Waltz"

There were more than three hundred song titles between the two collections, and each song was performed beautifully as the artists brought their stories to life, making them meaningful, spiritual, and magical all at the same time. Songs like "White Christmas" by Irving Berlin and "I'll Be Home for Christmas," both sung by Bing Crosby, were already nostalgic American classics having been made popular during WWII. Every song in Mom's collection provided a release from the real world, even a kid's real world, and evoked images of family, friends, romance, and the significance of a celebrated newborn Child-Savior-King.

Classics from other albums included:

Frank Sinatra – "The First Noel" / "I Believe" / "Mistletoe and Holly"
Nat King Cole – "The Christmas Song" / "Caroling, Caroling"
Elvis Presley – "I'll Be Home for Christmas" / "Blue Christmas"
Vince Guaraldi Trio – (Soundtrack to *A Charlie Brown Christmas*)
Burl Ives – (The singing snowman from *Rudolph the Red-Nosed Reindeer*)
Ella Fitzgerald – "Sleigh Ride"
Jimmy Durante – "Frosty the Snowman"
Louis Armstrong – "'Zat You, Santa Claus?"
Judy Garland – "Have Yourself a Merry Little Christmas"
Harry Belafonte – "I Heard the Bells on Christmas Day"

Rosemary Clooney – "Happy Christmas, Little Friend"
Dean Martin – "Baby, It's Cold Outside" / "I've Got My Love to Keep Me Warm"
Julie Andrews – "Joy to the World" / "The Bells of Christmas"
Lena Horne – "What Are You Doing New Year's Eve" / "Winter Wonderland"

Every year, as that pile of presents mounted, Mom reminded us that Christmas wasn't actually about the gifts under the tree, it was about the birth of Jesus first. But we didn't really need that reminder because the music constantly playing in our house wasn't just about toys and candy canes. Those songs had grown-up themes and painted the complete picture of the true meaning of the season, sparking a wide range of wonder and emotions along the way. To me, Doris Day's "Toyland" always felt a little seductive, and even I wanted to somehow meet up with that lady singing her torch song invitation to New Year's Eve, but I didn't know how to drive yet or where to even find her. That's not to say that we weren't all looking forward to our visit from Santa Claus, however. His arrival was, after all, the most anticipated event of the year.

By Christmas Eve we were are all a full month into mainlining Christmas Cheer so we'd wake up vibrating like caffeine fiends, pretty much clinically insane with anticipation. It was really too much, so we had to find ways to distract ourselves and I did that by either playing football outside or watching it on TV. Sometimes I'd go down to Bob's house to see what he was doing. One time we watched parts of an ultra-low-budget double feature in his room called *Santa Claus Conquers the Martians* and *Santa Claus vs The Devil*, the two most bizarre pieces of acid-tripping cinematography that I'd ever seen. We were monster movie aficionados and tuned into those movies out of curiosity, but luckily we only caught the second half of the first one and the first half of the second because after watching them we had to go outside to shake off the weirdness. They warned us about drug use in school and I believe those two movies entered my subconscious and kept me off the hard stuff. But there was no way I could concentrate on anything anyway, so by the time I got back home it was close to dinnertime and I'd lost the ability to form complete sentences or even feed myself. The countdown was on.

After dinner the table was cleared, all the dishes were cleaned and put away, the lights were turned out, and we were sent to our rooms to get ready for bed. And as the sun went down, the day turned to night, and the magic of Christmas Eve finally arrived to cast its spell. The house became quiet, the energy level subdued, and we returned to a living room that was illuminated only by the lights of the tree. It was time for Dad to read us, *The Night before Christmas*. He'd sit in a chair with all of us surrounding him, some sitting on the floor in front of him, some to his sides, some standing behind him looking over his shoulders, while the littlest ones sat on his lap their hands tugging on the book so they could see the pictures as he read.

'Twas the night before Christmas and all through the house,
Not a creature was stirring,
Not even a mouse.

Well, maybe a few mice. After Dad read the story, we were sent off to bed, but my brothers and I had planned to stay up all night to listen for Santa entering the house or to see if we could catch a glimpse of his elusive sleigh. We risked everything by doing this because we were told that Santa would not come to our house if we were awake, so we had to be *really* quiet. We had never pulled off an all-nighter, so we had to make preparations, which involved sneaking food and drinks into our room and hiding them during the day, for sustenance later. We also gathered flashlights with new batteries and readied our plastic Army binoculars so we could "spy to see if reindeer really know how to fly." We had a desk inset between two walls, so to kill some time I'd climb up on the desk and do my stand-up act while Dave and Landry shined their lights on me. I went on at 10:00 because I had a decent routine established at the time which included a comedy set followed by a short song and dance finale that really brought the house down. It also brought an angry Mom to our room. Unfortunately, by the time I finished and got in bed, it was only 10:10. We still had a long way to go, so we stayed up talking in whispers. Occasionally we heard a sound or a voice coming from downstairs, so we fell silent and listened. It was nothing. A little later one of us heard a bell sound coming from outside so we shushed ourselves and got up to look out the window to see what was the matter. We scanned the rooftops, but again it was nothing.

As hard as we tried to stay up, we were never able to pull it off, but because we did stay up so late, once we fell asleep, we slept soundly for what seemed like five minutes. Then, suddenly, we'd be startled awake to hear it: the horn blowing and Santa calling out, "Ho-Ho-Ho-MERRY CHRISTMAS!!!" and my dad in reply, "Good-bye, Santa Claus!" And then the living room door would slam shut. That was our signal. That was the green light to come downstairs and see what Santa brought us. He'd done it again! He got in and out without us seeing him! How did he do that? Shocked that we'd fallen asleep we would spring from our beds (the one and only day of the year that we sprang from our beds), bouncing off each other as we thundered down the wooden stairs like a herd of stampeding horses. Then we'd turn the corner and gaze upon the most magical sight: Toyland.

Christmas music would be playing softly, and the smell of coffee was in the air. Straight ahead, framed in the pocket doorway to the living room, was that big Christmas tree, lit up with those large old-school multicolored bulbs, with the light of the smaller twinkling bulbs lighting up the tinsel and flashing it onto all the shiny presents that surrounded it and filled the room. It was still dark outside and those were the only lights on in the house; they reflected off a train that sounded as it rolled around the track, off the silver handlebars of a yellow bike leaning against the wall. There were blue and red robot boxers standing in a ring, a doll peeking out of a box that leaned against a pink house standing in a corner, and board games propped up on chairs. The stack of wrapped presents under the tree gleamed and the scene cast a warm glow of color throughout the room and into our eyes, a sensory overload, that immediately cast us into its spell as we walked through the doorway...

Toyland, toyland
Little girl and boy land
While you dwell within it
You are ever happy there...

Santa created little areas in the living room for each kid where he displayed our presents. If there was any confusion, Mom and Dad would point us to our section, since they were there to see

Santa when he took off. I would enter the living room walking in a stupor, eyes boggled as I searched for my area, all of my senses still overwhelmed by the atmosphere. Once we all got settled Mom and Dad or Grandma would make hot chocolate for us while we played with our new toys.

Toyland, toyland
Little girl and boyland
Once you pass its borders
You can ne'er return again

All of the wrapped presents were still under the tree, but I never even looked at them because I was transfixed in the moment by the toys in front of me, and because we had a tradition about those wrapped presents.

Some of my friends opened their Christmas presents on Christmas Eve. Others would get to open one on Christmas Eve and the rest the next morning when they eventually woke up. That was unthinkable in our house. In our house, they had to be opened early on Christmas morning. Who would want it any other way when they could enter Toyland? So after Mom and Dad decided we had played enough, the opening of the wrapped presents would begin, with established protocol. Dad would pick out a present, read out the "To" and "From" names from the label, and pass the present to the recipient, upon which we would all watch them open it. Grandma, of course, divined hers prior to opening, but for the rest of us those presents were a complete surprise, some of them having been left under the tree by Santa! This process could take up to two hours, and by the time we finished the abused wrapping paper and ribbon would fill multiple lawn bags. After that Mom and Dad and the Big Girls would go back to bed, but if I could see the morning light coming through the windows, I was out the door to play with my new car or football until the other neighborhood kids came outside.

By the afternoon of Christmas Day, the fairy dusted portal would start to close, the spell would lift, and the world would begin to return to normal. In 1971 my favorite team, the Kansas City Chiefs, were playing my second favorite team, the Miami Dolphins, on Christmas Day. It was an epic battle that would go on to become the longest-lasting game in NFL history, ending with a Dolphin victory in double overtime, 27-24. That game started in the afternoon, and I had been watching it from the opening kickoff, until Mom called me to the table for dinner as evening settled in. The game was tied at 24 in the fourth quarter, so I didn't answer. The game was still tied at 24 in the first OT when she called me a second time. Again, I didn't answer, so she came into the living room and shut off the TV, which meant I missed the end of the game. It had been a great Christmas up until then, but after dinner I learned that the Chiefs had lost, so it became the worst Christmas Day ever. Obviously the Dolphins won because Mom turned off the TV and I wasn't able to finish the game. That's how your team loses; it's the way games work. There are some things Moms just don't understand.

Years later we started attending Midnight Mass on Christmas Eve, and there was one service that made me see Mom in a whole new light. I don't recall exactly how old I was, but we were in the post-Santa years and she sang in the choir at the time and was the featured soloist scheduled to sing "Ave Maria," a cappella. I could always make out her voice while she sang in the choir because it stood out, but this was the first time I'd heard her solo in church. That song, when sung properly, starts out softly and quietly, pianissimo, and when she started singing, the church quickly fell silent. Sung in Latin, "Ave Maria" is a very moving supplication that builds in volume and intensity as it progresses, and as my mother stood in front of the congregation her voice began to fill the church with a power and passion that I'd never heard from her, or witnessed anywhere for that matter. All of us had heard her sing at home, and neighbors could sometimes hear her voice from down the block, but this was different. As a congregation, we were hearing a sound that we'd never heard before in church. Her rendition moved me emotionally, a first as far as I can remember, and as she sang and the crescendo began to build people seated around me began to actually gasp. Her voice didn't just fill the church that night, it was as if the angels in heaven reached down through her and shook the building. This was the prodigy reborn. And when she finished there was silence. Silence. And then applause. Applause in a Catholic Church. Another first for me. I was in awe as I watched her sit down. Barbra Streisand sang the best version of "Ave Maria" that I had ever heard—until that night. Streisand's version wasn't even close to my mom's.

As time rolled on Mom and Dad hit their stride financially, and years later they moved into a new house that they had built in a new subdivision just outside of Houston's southwesterly city limits, in Sugar Land. By the time my nieces and nephews were teenagers they had friends whom they would invite to Mom and Dad's house on Christmas Day. Some were boyfriends or girlfriends, and some were strays who had nowhere else to go. The opening of the presents was now scheduled in the early afternoon, so those of us kids with families of our own could have their Christmas traditions first. If friends were expected, there would be a present under the tree for them, because it wasn't Christmas unless everybody had a present to open. If their visit was a surprise, somehow a wrapped present would appear on their lap.

Years later my nephew wrote, recorded, and produced one of my favorite Christmas songs called "Christmastime," a beautiful piece he composed when he was a young man that captured the memories and the true Christmas spirit he experienced growing up at Christmastime, when our family all gathered together at Mom and Dad's new house in Sugar Land. The song opens with just him, picking and lightly strumming on his guitar. After several bars the drums come in with a few intermittent downbeats and cymbal taps, and then the orchestration quietly enters to join him as he continues to play his guitar. And then it opens, with him singing alone:

The time of year is near,
Presents on the floor.
Please step inside my friend,
There's always room for more.
And I know Tradition rules the day,
Blameless some say we are.
The only thing that counts
Is what's in your heart,
And you love...
Yes you love...

Chris Garcia

The End of the Innocence

During my transition out of the Santa years I learned that my dad kept a horn hidden in a closet all year long. It was one of those plastic horns you blow at a birthday party or on New Year's Eve. At around the same time I learned that the Easter Bunny wasn't real. I found out about that on Easter Sunday when I caught the Big Girls hiding the eggs in our backyard. I was shocked. So I asked my dad if the Easter Bunny was real, and he answered me by saying, "No" and nothing else. I was at the sliding-glass door looking out into the backyard as he passed behind me and started up the stairs. Then I somehow connected the dots, and the horror struck me like a bolt of lightning. I turned and looked up the stairs with great trepidation and asked my dad: "Does that mean Santa isn't real either?" Without breaking stride or looking back he said, "Yep" and disappeared around the corner.

The 50s and its nostalgic sparkle were dulled, crushed, and left in ruins by the shifting tides of the 60s, which stripped away the innocence of the 50s and left a hard edge on a less hopeful nation. Chaos reigned in the 60s, and burn marks remained like scars on buildings, on streets, and in our hearts. It is perhaps the last time the spirit of Tom and Huck was alive in us, leading to outside adventures. Now they were grounded, locked indoors, or told to turn in their pocketknives and hide under desks.

The decade of the 60s was arguably one of the most volatile and divisive decades in our nation's history. It ushered in unprecedented exploration and the dawning of new science, new music, and new ideas that were not only crossing boundaries, they were moving the lines and recoloring them; those boundary crossings created a wedge driven into our culture, dividing the times and generations, and challenging the morality and faith that previously united the nation. In a single decade the US went from a country that looked like it had shifted from *American Graffiti* to the *Last Tango in Paris*. Our future was changing rapidly and by the early 70s, there was no chance at swimming against the rapidly changing tide.

In 1972, newspaper and TV reports started coming in about the strange and random disappearance of teenage boys from the streets of Houston. Within two years a man named Elmer Wayne Henley, the personification of pure evil, was arrested for the cold-blooded killing of his partner-in-crime, Dean Corll, and sent to prison shortly thereafter for his participation in the kidnap, torture, and assault on twenty-eight known victims in what became known as the Houston Mass Murders, described then as, "the deadliest case of serial murders in American history."

Right around that same time, Ronald Clark O'Bryan, a man from Pasadena, Texas, located just on the outskirts of southeast Houston, shocked the nation when he was charged with murdering his own son on Halloween night by lacing the eight-year-old's Pixy Stix with cyanide. He became known as The

Candyman, and The Man who Killed Halloween. But these events took place in the early 70s, towards the very end of my trick-or-treating years.

America was rocked by the manifestation of this new brand of monster who preyed on the innocent, on children, and Houston was at ground zero, gripped in fear. The dark spirit of a wicked purveyor of evil was suddenly woven into our nation's fabric, slamming the brakes on our night games, and eventually ending Halloween as we knew it, forever.

I saw the headlines and heard the news, but I was still just a kid, and one who knew that these things were swirling around me. What I didn't know then was that, for better or for worse, America was going through some big adjustments, or serious growing pains—whichever way you saw it—and you just had to grab hold of something around you that was solid and true and hang on to it for the ride. But whether things turned out for better or worse the changes presented a problem: the left fought the right, and the right fought the left, and instead of arriving at solutions they created chaos—a chaos that shook foundations and left all unsettled. It seems like we're still hanging on to this day for that dark ride towards the waterfall.

So what do we do? There's no looking back now; Tom and Huck are gone forever. The only thing we can do is look forward. Since nobody can come up with the right answers, maybe we should just close our eyes and let Captain Bob's wisdom take the helm and drive us right through it.

But the news wasn't all bad in the early 70s. My sister Cindy started dating a guy in 1973 who rode a motorcycle and looked like Gregg Allman. Mom and Dad had to meet him first, so before their first date he came to our house to properly introduce himself. As soon as he walked through our living room Grandma Garcia sat him down at our dining room table and served him her tortillas and beans. We were never able to get rid of him after that. Eventually Mom would go for a ride on the back of his motorcycle and the next year Cindy married him. Cindy was the first to leave our house, but her story with Greg (that's really his name), continues.

As well as I knew Bob, it's a little disconcerting how little I knew my brothers and sisters back then. Like I said in the beginning, I wasn't paying much attention. It's no wonder, really, because as a kid, I was running everywhere I went. I think all kids do that. I mean, unless a kid is out with their parents, when do you ever see them just *walking*? Whether they're inside or outside, they're running. But that's what parents tell them to do: run upstairs to bed, run down to the Layton's, run along now—we were always running. It's hard to see what's going on around you when you're in constant flight.

But when we weren't running, there were so many things we did as a family. Sometimes Mom and Dad would cram us kids all together in the station wagon for a movie night at Loew's Drive-In Theater, or for a day trip to San Antonio so Grandma could stock up on her Mexican cookies and bread. That's eleven people in one vehicle for a three-hour trip one way. We went to church together every Sunday and sat together every night for dinner. We celebrated victories together and suffered through losses together.

It was my brothers and sisters whom I sat with in the front yard to pull a blade of grass from the lawn, to put it between our thumbs, and to blow on it until we were dizzy to see if we could make it whistle. Sometimes we would lie on our backs during the day to take a break and rest, listening as the Gulf winds rustled the leaves above us and as they combed softly through the trees; and looking up beyond the swaying tree line to the blue sky above as the clouds sailed slowly by, like an armada of puffy white ships at sea, naming them horse or clown as they dissipated, or sailed away like misty spirits drifting out of sight and into the kaleidoscope looking glass of our Carvel Daze.

Epilogue

During the writing of this book I shared the Buster Willis chapter with Bob and his brother Bill, not telling them about the book but passing the writing off as an essay I was goofing on. A few days later Bill texted me, "I conveniently forgot about the sidewalk tackles and thorn bushes somehow. I guess if we could survive Carvel the rest of the ride was downhill and shady!" I texted back that it was easy to forget when you weren't on the receiving end.

Bob and I huddled together at the side of The Red Barn when we were kids and drew blood on our palms with a knife and shook hands, to become blood brothers. There's no doubt we saw that in a movie we watched together, and through the years we continued to notch new memories. We ended up playing together one year on the Indians baseball team, and later we roomed together in college. We camped and vacationed together with our friends and attended concerts and ball games together, including a trip to Minute Maid Park with Bill to watch the Astros defeat the Boston Red Sox in Game 6 to clinch the American League Championship Series and move on to the World Series in 2021. During and after our college years, our group of friends would regularly meet in the backyard of his parents' house down the street from me, where we'd buy a keg of beer on a Friday afternoon and return it empty the next Monday. He turned out to be the hub in our group of friends that I eventually referred to as The Carvel Gang.

On December 8, 2021, I finished writing this book and told Sharon that I wanted to give it to our sibs and to Bob as a Christmas present, so we got busy editing and developing a working copy. Around Thanksgiving I told my family about the book, but I hadn't had a chance to tell Bob. Shortly after I completed the writing, he and I booked our annual Christmas dinner at Los Tios with my neighbors, the Duncans, for December 18. My plan was to tell him about the book on the way to dinner. At 5:15 p.m. on Saturday, the 18th Bob called me to say that he'd just gotten out of the shower and that, "I'll be ready to go in five, Pardner, so shoot on by." His house was only blocks away from mine, and as I drove there to pick him up I was amped up about telling him that I had written a book. I wasn't going to tell him what role he played in it; I just wanted to give him the title and an overall idea of the book, tell him that it was finished, and then surprise him with the working draft as his Christmas present. I knew he would be equally excited to hear about it.

At 5:22 p.m. I pulled into his driveway and honked, our normal pick-up call. He didn't come out, so after a minute or two I gave the horn another toot and he still didn't come out. I figured getting ready was taking longer than expected but after a couple of more minutes he still hadn't appeared, so I texted him then called him to let him know that I was in the driveway. When he didn't answer I became concerned and rang the doorbell and knocked on his door. Still no answer. So I checked the doorknob and a couple of windows, but everything was locked. By now the

Duncans had called from the restaurant asking about our whereabouts, and after I told them about my growing concern they told me they were on their way over. I went around his house checking all the doors and windows, calling out his name as I tried to get in. The Duncans arrived just as I broke in through his bedroom window and threw open his blinds to find him in a heap on the floor. I was too late. He was gone. It was evident that he had passed right after hanging up the phone with me.

Bob's death was an earthquake. The hearts of hundreds of people were leveled upon hearing about his passing. His loss was too soon and too big to comprehend. His heart was too big to comprehend. He was the first person I talked to when we moved here, and I was the last person he talked to when he left here. Think about that. The name of that song from *The Defiant Ones* is "Long Gone." It means something. This all means something. I just haven't figured out what it is yet.

Bob is gone now. But the Shipley Do-Nut shop across the street from Bayland Park and the Baskin-Robbins down the same street still remain. Most of my brothers and sisters remain here, too, having spread out around town, and we all remain close, circling the wagons should a crisis ever arise, but we still haven't found Mexican food that rivals Grandma Garcia's anywhere. Mom and Dad have passed but the house on Carvel Lane is still there, with me and that scorched closet in it, but the neighborhood trees matured so the soft glow of the stadium lights can no longer be seen in the summertime. You certainly can't hear the roar of the crowd anymore, because there is no crowd. They aged, the demographics changed, and most of them either died or moved on. I still ride my bike around the park for exercise, but the baseball fields are no longer full of activity, some having been replaced by a couple of more girls softball fields, a couple of geezer softball fields, and with the biggest change being the addition of a couple of soccer fields. That "Field of My Dreams" is gone now, just a faded twinkling memory. But maybe Terrence Mann was right when he said, *"America has rolled by like an army of steamrollers. . . . But baseball has marked the time. . . . It reminds us of all that once was good, and it could be again."*

I hope so.

This book is also dedicated to My First Friend, Bob. May his memory and great spirit continue to live in all of the people who knew him and loved him.

Bowling Gree—*een!*

CARVEL DAZE

Carvel Daze Songs Playlist

Disc1
Carry On - Crosby, Stills, Nash & Young
Suite: Judy Blue Eyes - Crosby, Stills & Nash
Marrakesh Express - Crosby, Stills & Nash
A Horse With No Name - America
Love The One You're With - Stephen Stills
Diamond Girl - Seals & Crofts
Summer Breeze - Seals & Crofts
No Sugar Tonight - The Guess Who
No Time - The Guess Who
She's Come Undone - The Guess Who
These Eyes - The Guess Who
From The Beginning - Emerson, Lake & Palmer
Beginnings - Chicago
Does Anybody Really Know What Time It Is? - Chicago
Saturday Night - Chicago
Spinning Wheel - Blood, Sweat & Tears
You've Made Me So Very Happy - Blood, Sweat & Tears

Carvel Daze Songs Playlist

Disc2
Let's Stay Together - Al Green
Backstabbers - O'Jays
Love Train - O'Jays
Me & Mrs. Jones - Billy Paul
Nothing From Nothing - Billy Preston
Really Go Round in Circles - Billy Preston
Whatcha See Is Whatcha Get - The Dramatics
Midnight Train To Georgia - Gladys Knight & The Pips
Rubber Band Man - The Spinners
Could It Be I'm Falling In Love - The Spinners
I'll Be Around - The Spinners
O-o-h Child - The Five Stairsteps
Ain't No Mountain High Enough - Diana Ross & The Supremes
Stop In The Name of Love - The Supremes
You Keep Me Hangin' On - The Supremes
Ain't No Woman Like The One I've Got - Four Tops
Get Ready - Rare Earth
Brandy - Looking Glass
Take A Letter Maria - R. B. Greaves
Vehicle - The Ides of March
Shaft - Isaac Hayes
Mercy, Mercy Me - Marvin Gaye

Chris Garcia

About the Author

Chris Garcia was born in Kansas City and raised in Texas: "good cowboy stock" as he likes to put it, which means he knows something about barbecue and how to smoke a brisket. It does not mean, however, that he knows how to cowboy.

Published once previously on the cover of *Inside Houston* Magazine, he waited until now to publish again, waking on the back nine from a very deep sleep and teeing this book up as he plays out the tail end of his round. His golf game is a little rusty these days, so take shelter everyone because after long breaks, this man has actually driven balls into the windshields of two moving vehicles.